English Works

2

**John Catron,
Chris Marshall
and Jo Shackleton**

Hodder & Stoughton

A MEMBER OF THE HODDER HEADLINE GROUP

Copyright text
Unit 1 p. 2. 'At Home, Abroad' by Jackie Kay from *The Frog who Dreamed She was an Opera Singer*, Bloomsbury 1998; p. 5 © BBC; p. 6 'Duncan Gets Expelled' by Jackie Kay from *Two's Company*, Puffin 1994; p. 8 'Attention Seeking' by Jackie Kay from *The Nation's Favourite Poems of Childhood*, BBC Worldwide; p. 10 'Stressed Out' by Jackie Kay from *The Frog who Dreamed She was an Opera Singer*, Bloomsbury 1998; p. 18 'Brendon Gallacher' by Jackie Kay from *Two's Company*, Puffin 1994; pp. 20 and 22 from *The Adoption Papers* by Jackie Kay, Bloodaxe Books 1991. **Unit 2** p. 33 © BBC Online, 8 January 2002; pp. 37 and 41 extract from *TXT TLK* by Chantelle Horton, The Chicken House 2001; p. 38 © Paul Crozier for Mirror.co.uk, 1 February 2002; p. 40 © Charles Shoebridge for *The Guardian*, 8 January 2002. **Unit 3** all extracts from *Holes* by Louis Sachar, Bloomsbury. **Unit 4** p. 93 extract from *Zlata's Diary: A Child's Life in Sarajevo* by Zlata Filipovic, translated by Christina Pribichevich-Zori (Viking 1994, first published in France as *Le Journal de Zlata* by Fixot et editions Robert Laffont 1993) © Fixot et editions Robert Laffont 1993.

Copyright photographs:
p. 1 © Ingrid Pollard/Bloodaxe Books; p. 2 (top) © Cliff Threadgold/Life File Photo Library, (bottom) © Barbara Berkowitz/Life File Photo Library; p. 5 © Brian Mitchell/Photofusion; p. 15 (left) © Jacky Chapman/Photofusion, (right) © CORBIS; p. 22 © Getty Images Inc; p. 24 © Getty; p. 29 © Royalty-Free/CORBIS; p. 31 © Ulrike Preuss/Photofusion; p. 44 Paul Baldesare/Photofusion; p. 46 © Emma Lee/Life File Photo Library; p. 47 covers of *Holes* by Louis Sachar supplied by Bloomsbury; p. 61 and 65 © William Manning/CORBIS; p. 70 © Dr Morley Read/Science Photo Library; p. 72 (both photos) © Joe McDonald/Bruce Coleman Collection; p. 77 all © Topham Picturepoint; p. 91 © Topham Picturepoint; p. 93 © Topham Picturepoint; p. 110 © David Parker/Science Photo Library; p. 111 © Charles & Josette Lenars/CORBIS; p. 122 © MTV Europe Music Awards 2001; p. 124 © Ulrike Preuss/Photofusion; p. 129 (left) © John Fitzgerald Kennedy Library, Boston, (middle) © Central Press, (right) © PA News Photo Library; p. 131 © Smith Collection, Smith College; p. 133 © CORBIS; p. 136 © Charles O'Rear/CORBIS; p. 141 © IWM; p. 142 © Mark Taylor/Life File Photo Library; p. 143 © Michael Nicholson/CORBIS.

Illustrations:
pp. 7, 8, 10, 12, 18, 39, 49, 54, 56, 59, 69, 96, 99, 105, 108 by Ben Hasler.
pp. 20, 26, 50, 64, 80, 82, 86, 89, 94, 114, 116 by Ruth Thomlevold.

Contributors:
Unit 1: Nisha Tank
Unit 2: Su Bank and Sue Haigh
Unit 3: Hayley Davies-Edwards
Unit 4: Jean Moore
Unit 5: Lucy Lawrence
Unit 6: Andrew McCallum
Unit 7: Frances Gregory
Unit 8: Jo Shackleton

Every effort has been made to trace copyright holders of material reproduced in this book. Any rights not acknowledged here will be acknowledged in subsequent printings if notice is given to the publisher.

Orders: please contact Bookpoint Ltd, 130 Milton Park, Abingdon, Oxon OX14 4SB. Telephone: (44) 01235 827720. Fax: (44) 01235 400454. Lines are open from 9.00–6.00, Monday to Saturday, with a 24 hour message answering service. You can also order through our website www.hodderheadline.co.uk.

British Library Cataloguing in Publication Data
A catalogue record for this title is available from the British Library

ISBN 0 340 87252 7

First Published 2003
Impression number   10 9 8 7 6 5 4 3 2 1
Year   2007 2006 2005 2004 2003

Copyright © 2003 John Catron, Chris Marshall and Jo Shackleton

Cover photo from Imagebank/Getty.
Typeset by Pantek Arts Ltd, Maidstone, Kent, ME14 1NY
Printed in Italy for Hodder & Stoughton Educational, a division of Hodder Headline, 338 Euston Road, London NW1 3BH.

Contents

UNIT 1 — Let's face it! The poetry of Jackie Kay

In this unit you will learn about the following key objectives:

Development of key ideas – looking at how a writer develops her ideas through the way she organises and writes her poems

Interpret a text – working out your own interpretation of what a poem means and how it is written

Hypothesis and speculation – using talk to develop your thinking about ideas

As you work through this unit you will read a selection of poems by the contemporary poet Jackie Kay. You will also study some poems written before 1900 and explore how they are linked with the modern poems through the themes and issues with which they deal.

This unit will teach you to become a critical and reflective reader, someone who reads between the lines and questions what they are reading. You will learn how to use talk to ask questions about the text that you are reading, probing and challenging ideas and viewpoints. You will find out about how to hypothesise and speculate – use talk to explore possible meanings and offer new ideas.

Through your reading of the poems you will learn how to analyse a text. You will explore how writers develop their ideas through the way that they organise their poems and through the language that they use. By completing a variety of spoken, reading and writing activities you will learn how to comment on a poet's particular choice of structure, language and themes, and how these affect you, the reader. Your final task will be to write a formal essay about two poems.

Jackie Kay was born in Scotland in 1961. She had a white Scottish mother and black Nigerian father. She was adopted by a white Scottish couple and brought up in Glasgow. In the poem 'At Home, Abroad', Jackie Kay explores the mixture of her Scottish and Nigerian background.

At Home, Abroad

All summer
I dream of
places I've never
been
where I might
see faces
I've never seen,
like the dark
face of my
father in
Nigeria,
or the pale
face of my
mother in
the Highlands,
or the bright
faces of my
cousins at
Land's End.

All summer
I spell the names
of tricky countries
just in case
I get a sudden
invite: Madagascar,
Cameroon. I draw
cartoons of
airports, big and small.
Who will meet me?
Will they
shake hands or
kiss both cheeks?
I draw
duty frees
with every
country's favourite
sweetie, smiling
a sugary welcome,
and myself,
cap-peaked,
wondering if I am
'home'.

TASK

❶ In pairs, discuss how Jackie Kay feels about not knowing her birth mother and father.

❷ What techniques does she use as a writer to get across her thoughts and feelings?

Working in pairs, consider:

- How Jackie Kay uses words and punctuation to suggest her own uncertainty about her background
- Why she repeats certain words and phrases
- Why she organises the poem into two **stanzas**
- The use of setting
- The use of contrasting language, e.g. 'pale' and 'dark'

When talking through ideas, you will be hypothesising and speculating. The following talk toolkits will help you in both your pair discussion and in reporting back to the class:

I think ...
This suggests ...
I wonder ...
I guess ...
I suppose ...
It can ...
It may ...
It might ...

Probably ...
Possibly ...
Maybe ...
Perhaps ...
Presumably ...
What if ...?
What about ...?

Stanza: Poets often divide their poems into groups of lines called stanzas. Stanzas are separated from each other by a space in the printed text.

You will read a number of poems in this unit. In order to record your responses and ideas you will need to keep a reading journal.

Write your first entry about how you responded to the poem 'At Home, Abroad'.

To help you organise your ideas and responses, use the ideas below:

Reading journal — Prompt sheet

Poem: 'At Home, Abroad' by Jackie Kay

Subject: What do you think the poem is about? Give some evidence to support you ideas.

Structure: How is the poem organised? How effective is this?

Style: Comment on how the poet uses language to express her ideas. Give some examples. What is the effect?

Technique: What techniques does the poet use? Give some examples. What is the effect?

Links with other poems: Do the themes, ideas and techniques used in this poem link with any other poems you have studied? Give examples.

Overall comment: This is your personal response to the poem. What are your thoughts, ideas and views?

Useful vocabulary

- Key themes
- Imagery
- Line length
- Vocabulary choices
- Language patterns
- Repetition
- Contrast
- Structure
- Viewpoint
- Values

Useful sentence starters

- My first impressions of … were … because …
- I then thought … because …
- At this point … because …
- The poet uses … to …
- The effect of this is …
- I have noticed …
- This is linked to … because …
- My personal response is …

Jackie Kay often draws on her own experiences as inspiration for her poetry writing. Below is an extract from an interview with her that was published on the BBC News Scotland website. In the article Jackie Kay talks about how, as a child, she was the victim of bullying and that this prompted her to write 'little poems of revenge'.

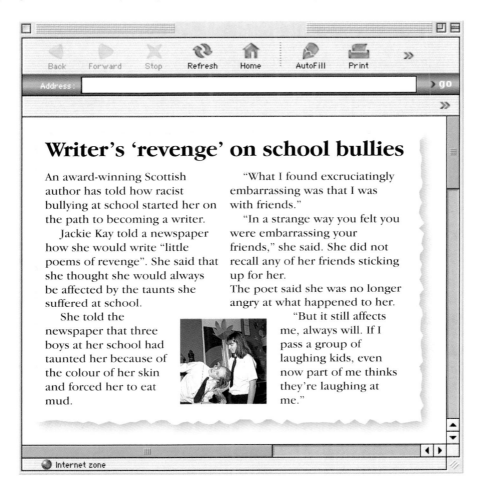

Writer's 'revenge' on school bullies

An award-winning Scottish author has told how racist bullying at school started her on the path to becoming a writer.

Jackie Kay told a newspaper how she would write "little poems of revenge". She said that she thought she would always be affected by the taunts she suffered at school.

She told the newspaper that three boys at her school had taunted her because of the colour of her skin and forced her to eat mud.

"What I found excruciatingly embarrassing was that I was with friends."

"In a strange way you felt you were embarrassing your friends," she said. She did not recall any of her friends sticking up for her.

The poet said she was no longer angry at what happened to her.

"But it still affects me, always will. If I pass a group of laughing kids, even now part of me thinks they're laughing at me."

TASK

❶ How did Jackie Kay feel about being bullied? How does she feel now?

❷ Record your comments in a table like the one below:

How she felt/feels now	Evidence
Embarrassed	She felt embarrassed in front of her friends

One of Jackie Kay's poems describes being bullied at primary school. The poem is about one particular boy who made her break times a misery. The name she gives the bully in this poem was not the real bully's name.

Duncan Gets Expelled

There are three big boys from primary seven
who wait at the main school gate with stones
in their teeth and names in their pockets.
Every day the three big boys are waiting.
'There she is. Into her boys. Hey Sambo.'

I dread the bell ringing, and the walk home.
My best friend is scared of them and runs off.
Some days they shove a mud pie into my mouth.
'That's what you should eat,' and make me eat it.
Then they all look in my mouth, prodding a stick.

I'm always hoping we get detention.
I'd love to write 'I will be better' 400 times.
The things I do? I pull Agnes MacNamara's hair.
Or put a ruler under Rhona's bum and ping it back
till she screams; or I make myself sick in the toilet.

Until the day the headmaster pulls me out,
asking all about the three big boys.
I'm scared to open my mouth.
But he says, 'you can tell me, is it true?'
So out it comes, making me eat the mud pies.

Two of them got lines for the whole of May.
But he got expelled, that Duncan MacKay.

Jackie Kay often uses her own experiences in her poetry. She says, 'If I got called names, I could go away and write a poem about some terrible revenge. Your imagination allows you to survive in a completely different way.'

TASK

❶ Working in a group, discuss how Jackie Kay uses both her imagination and skill as a poet to make the experience of being bullied really frightening and threatening in 'Duncan Gets Expelled'. Explore:
  ❑ The words and imagery used to describe the boys' physical appearance
  ❑ The use of dialogue: what they say
  ❑ Words that describe her own and other pupils' fear of these boys
  ❑ Her own behaviour in school
❷ The last stanza describes what happens to the bullies. In what tone of voice would you read these lines?
❸ What advice would you give to people of your own age who are being bullied? Make a list of helpful suggestions.
❹ Share your group's suggestions with the rest of the class. Agree a class list of the five most helpful pieces of advice.

HEAD OF YEAR 8

A number of Jackie Kay's poems are about the difficulties of growing up. Her poem 'Attention Seeking' is all about the lengths a boy goes to in order to get attention. However, the poem also gives us some clues about why the boy behaves in this way.

Attention Seeking

I'm needing attention.
I know I'm needing attention
because I hear people say it.
People that know these things.
I'm needing attention,
so what I'll do is steal something.
I know I'll steal something
because that is what I do
when I'm needing attention.
Or else I'll mess up my sister's room,
throw all her clothes onto the floor,
put her gerbil under her pillow
and lay a trap above the door
a big heavy dictionary to drop on her
when she comes through. (Swot.)
This is the kind of thing I do
when I'm needing attention.

But I'm never boring.
I always think up new things.
Attention has lots of colours
and tunes. And lots of punishments.
For attention you can get detention.
Extra homework. Extra housework.
All sorts of things. Although
yesterday I heard the woman say
That I was just needing
someone to listen. My dad went mad.
'Listen to him!' he said 'Listen!
You've got to be joking.'
Mind you that was right after
I stole his car keys and drove
his car straight into the wall.
I wasn't hurt, but I'm still
needing quite a lot of attention.

TASK

The poet is really trying hard to grab the reader's attention. How does she manage to do this? In pairs, consider:

- The subject matter
- The techniques that the poet uses to engage your attention
- How a strong viewpoint is conveyed
- Your response as a reader

Use the prompts opposite to help you discuss your ideas. Remember to always provide evidence to support your thinking, e.g. quotations from the poem.

Reading poetry? Use these prompts to help you ask the right questions and get thinking.

Who is the narrator or teller of this poem?
What is the tone of the poem? Does it change?
Do the line lengths vary? What is the effect?
Are the lines statements, questions, exclamations? What effects do they create?
Are certain words/phrases/ideas emphasised? Why?
Are there any examples of particularly dramatic vocabulary?
Are there examples of powerful verbs?
Are words used in unusual ways?
Can you see any patterns in the language?
How does the poet create images? Use of simile, metaphor, personification?
How does the poet create sound? Use of alliteration and onomatopoeia?
Is dialogue used? If so, why?
Are there hints or suggestions that make you want to ask questions?
Can you work out the intended effect on the audience?
How does the style influence your reading, understanding and appreciation?
Does this have any connection to previous poems you have read?

The poem 'Stressed Out' by Jackie Kay also presents some of the difficulties that teenagers face at school and at home.

Stressed Out

I am totally stressed out.
I can't sleep at night.
I shake when I hear them shout.
He has his nerve pills; she has her alcohol.

Me? I have nothing at all.
There is no one to talk to.
I have this strange singing in my head.
At night, alone in bed,

The stress is in my sheets,
clinging to my nightdress,
climbing in through the windows.
There are tests tomorrow;

bullies posted in the playground.
Many things to remember.
I told my mother: I said,
'I am totally stressed out.'

She said, 'Don't be silly
Children don't get stressed.'
'Like Hell they don't,' I said.
And she sent me to my room for swearing.

So now here I am,
stuck in my stupid bedroom,
locked up, stressed out, all alone.
I swear to bring my stress levels down.

Life sucks.

TASK

❶ In pairs, read the poem.
❷ Using the prompts from page 9, select five questions you would like to ask about the poem.

TASK

❶ Exchange the questions that you have selected with another pair.

❷ In your own pair, answer the questions you have been given. Remember to give evidence to support your ideas. You will be asked to explain your answers to the pair who gave you the questions.

❸ Join up with the pair you gave your questions to and explain your ideas and opinions about them.

❹ The talk toolkit below contains useful phrases to help you develop your thinking and explore your ideas and views. Use these in your discussion.

> Use questions to open up a discussion by offering a suggestion, e.g. 'What about ...?'

> Draw someone else into the discussion, e.g. 'So what do you think?'

Get involved! Involve others!

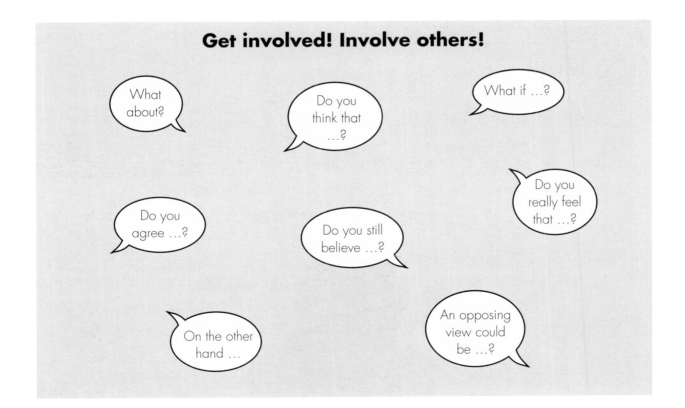

What's your problem?

❶ In groups, discuss what advice you would give to the narrator in the poem 'Stressed Out'.

❷ Share your ideas with the rest of the class.

❸ Imagine that you are the teenager in Jackie Kay's poem 'Stressed Out'. Write a letter to an agony aunt telling her what your problems are and asking for advice.

Dear Deirdre,

Things have got so bad that I don't know who else to turn to. I am totally stressed out!

Firstly, I can't sleep at night and keep breaking out in these horrible sweats. I'm sure that it is the stress that is causing it!

What's more ...

As if that's not bad enough ...

Jackie Kay's poems often describe the difficulties of growing up in today's society. However, the theme of youth is not a new one. William Shakespeare, writing over 400 years ago, discusses the same issue in his poem 'Age and Youth'. He presents a much more positive view of being young. He portrays youth as an exciting and energetic time, when you enjoy good health and have a spirit of adventure.

Age and Youth

Crabbed age and youth cannot live together,
Youth is full of pleasance, Age is full of care,
Youth like summer morne, Age like winter weather,
Youth like summer brave, Age like winter bare.
Youth is full of sport, Age's breath is short,
Youth is nimble, Age is lame,
Youth is hot and bold, Age is weake and cold,
Youth is wild, and Age is tame.
   Age I doe abhor thee, Youth I doe adore thee,
      O my love, my love is young:
   Age I doe defie thee. Oh sweet Shepheard hie thee:
      For methinks thou stay'st too long.

William Shakespeare

TASK

In this poem, Shakespeare contrasts being young and being old.

❶ How does he use language to create images of being young and old? What sort of images does he use:
  ❏ to describe being young?
  ❏ to describe being old?
❷ Are the images linked in any way?
❸ What do you think the benefits are of being young? How do you imagine yourself when you are much older?
❹ Write your own poem contrasting age and youth. When drafting it:
  ❏ use Shakespeare's structure, repeating the words 'age' and 'youth' for emphasis
  ❏ keep the lines short
  ❏ make sure that you use contrasting images
  ❏ try to link your images.

The poet Elizabeth Barrett Browning lived in the 1800s. She was the eldest of 12 children and came from a wealthy family. However, in her poem 'Child Labour' she describes the life of children much less fortunate than herself.

From *Child Labour*

"For oh," say the children, "we are weary
And we cannot run or leap;
If we cared for any meadows, it were merely
To drop down in them and sleep.
Our knees tremble sorely in the stooping,
We fall upon our faces, trying to go;
And underneath our heavy eyelids drooping
The reddest flower would look as pale as snow.
For, all day, we drag our burden tiring
Through the coal-dark, underground;
Or, all day, we drive the wheels of iron
In the factories, round and round.

"For all day the wheels are droning, turning;
Their wind comes in our faces,
Till our hearts turn, our heads with pulses burning,
And the walls turn in their places:
Turns the sky in the high window, blank and reeling,
Turns the long light that drops adown the wall,
Turn the black flies that crawl along the ceiling:
All are turning, all the day, and we with all.
And all day, the iron wheels are droning,
And sometimes we could pray,
'O ye wheels' (breaking out in a mad moaning)
'Stop! be silent for to-day!'"

TASK

For this task, work in a pair using a copy of the poem 'Child Labour'.
Highlight all the words and phrases that emphasise the hardship and **drudgery** of the life of children working in the coal mine. Look for:

● Descriptions of the setting
● How the children are described
● What the children say
● How the poet emphasises that the work seems endless
● How the poet suggests that the situation will not improve

Drudgery: hard, menial or dull work

Both Jackie Kay and Elizabeth Barrett Browning describe some of the difficulties faced by young people. However, the problems faced by children in the 1800s are very different to the problems faced by young people today.

TASK

❶ Look back at the notes you made in your reading journal about Jackie Kay's poems.

❷ Working in a pair and using a copy of the table below, make a list of all the issues and problems facing young people that Jackie Kay deals with in her poems.

❸ Repeat this for the poem by Elizabeth Barrett Browning. What differences do you notice? How do you explain them?

Jackie Kay	Elizabeth Barrett Browning
Being bullied	Exhaustion

You don't believe me, do you?

❚❚ It's a huge freedom to be allowed to make things up in your head. I always loved that as a kid. I used to make up terrible lies. I liked seeing whether or not I could be believed. ❚❚ Jackie Kay

What is the difference between 'making things up' and lying? In this part of the unit you will be asked to state your opinion and make a judgement about this question.

TASK

❶ Why do you think people make things up or lie?

❷ What sort of things do people lie about?

❸ Below is a list of things people might lie about. Working in groups, put them in rank order, with the most serious lie at the top and the least serious at the bottom.

As you carry out this task, remember you are being asked to state your opinion or make a judgement. In other words you are being asked to evaluate ideas. Use some of the words or phrases in the talk toolkit on page 17 to help you in your discussion.

Telling your teacher that you have lost your homework when you have not done it
Telling your mum that you are staying at a friend's house when really you are at an all-night party
Telling your dad that your baby brother spilt coffee on his CD player, when really it was you
Taking money from your mum's purse and denying it
Telling your parents you have done well in an exam when you haven't
Telling your dad that you've walked the dog when you haven't
Pretending you're ill so that you don't have to go to school and do the French test
Telling your mum that you've got a 'bad hand' to avoid doing the washing-up
Lying to the police about where you were on Saturday night
Pretending that you are older than you really are
Telling everyone that your cousin is a millionaire

Offer statements of opinion or judgement

In my opinion …

I think …

I prefer …

I would rather …

Compare and constrast

Compared with …

Similarly …

Alternatively …

On the other hand …

Despite …

Use causal connectives

Because …

Therefore …

In that case …

Still …

Even though …

Consequently …

As a result …

Use adjectives and determiners to compare

Better

Best

Most

More

Worst

Less

Least

Helpful verbs

Prefer

Would rather

Like/dislike

In Jackie Kay's own childhood, she had an imaginary friend called Brendon Gallacher. He is the subject of one of her poems.

Brendon Gallacher (For my brother Maxie)

He was seven and I was six, my Brendon Gallacher.

He was Irish and I was Scottish, my Brendon Gallacher.

His father was in prison; he was a cat burglar.

My father was a communist party full-time worker.

He had six brothers and I had one, my Brendon Gallacher.

He would hold my hand and take me by the river

Where we'd talk all about his family being poor.

He'd get his mum out of Glasgow when he got older.

A wee holiday someplace nice. Some place far.

I'd tell my mum about my Brendon Gallacher

How his mum drank and his daddy was a cat burglar.

And she'd say, 'why not have him round to dinner?'

No, no, I'd say he's got big holes in his trousers.

I like meeting him by the burn in the open air.

Then one day after we'd been friends two years,

One day when it was pouring and I was indoors,

My mum says to me, 'I was talking to Mrs Moir

Who lives next door to your Brendon Gallacher

Didn't you say his address was 24 Novar?

She says there are no Gallachers at 24 Novar

There never have been any Gallachers next door.'

And he died then, my Brendon Gallacher,

Flat out on my bedroom floor, his spiky hair,

His impish grin, his funny flapping ear.

Oh Brendon, Oh my Brendon Gallacher.

TASK

Jackie Kay describes her imaginary friend as someone who is exciting but also someone who arouses our sympathy as a reader.

❶ What techniques does she use in the poem 'Brendon Gallacher' to create this effect on the reader? Consider:
- ❏ How she describes Brendon
- ❏ How she describes his family
- ❏ The way in which she compares him to herself

❷ Working in pairs, discuss and make notes on the following questions:
- ❏ How do you think the narrator feels when her pretence is found out? Look for evidence in the poem – the narrator does not tell us directly but we can read between the lines.
- ❏ What do you think the writer means by the line 'And then he died, my Brendon Gallacher'?
- ❏ Do you think that the narrator should be punished for making things up? Why?

Some of Jackie Kay's most serious poems are those that deal with the issue of adoption. You will remember that she had a Scottish mother and a Nigerian father but was adopted as a baby by a white Scottish couple. Jackie wrote a collection of poems entitled *The Adoption Papers*, which tells the story of a black girl's adoption by a white Scottish couple. The story is told from three different viewpoints: the daughter, the mother and the birth mother.

Jackie Kay won two prizes for this collection of poems. Some of the poems have also been broadcast on television and radio.

Below is the part of the poem which describes an imaginary meeting between the daughter and her birth mother. The words in bold are the voice of the birth mother. The rest is the voice of the daughter.

From *The Adoption papers*

She is faceless
She had no nose
She is five foot eight inches tall
She likes hockey best
She is twenty-six today
She was a waitress
My hair is grey
She wears no particular dress
The skin around my neck is wrinkling
Does she imagine me this way?
Lately I make pictures of her
But I can see the smallness
She is tall and slim
of her hands, Yes

Her hair is loose curls
an opal stone on her middle finger
I reach out to catch her
Does she talk broad Glasgow?
But no matter how fast
Maybe they moved years ago
I run after
She is faceless, she never
weeps. She has neither eyes nor
fine boned cheeks
Once would be enough,
just to listen to her voice
watch the way she moves her hands
when she talks.

TASK

❶ Read the statement cards about this poem. You will need to decide whether you agree with them or not.

❷ Working in a group, discuss where to place the statements on your copy of the grid. You must draw on evidence from the poem to support your ideas. Refer back to the talk toolkit on page 17, which gives you words and phrases to express an opinion or judgement. These will help you to carry out this task effectively.

The poem is about a woman with a deformed face
The daughter finds it hard to imagine her birth mother
The birth mother is portrayed as a tough woman
The birth mother thinks about her daughter who she gave up for adoption
The birth mother regrets giving her baby up
The birth mother imagines what her daughter is like
The daughter wants to find out about her birth mother
The daughter makes up details about her birth mother
A lot of time has passed since the birth mother gave her baby up for adoption
The daughter would be satisfied to meet her birth mother just once
The birth mother is to blame
The daughter should give up looking for her birth mother
The daughter should never give up looking for her birth mother

Definitely	Probably
Unsure	Definitely not

In the following poem from *The Adoption Papers*, the daughter has obtained the number of her birth mother's mother, i.e. her grandmother. She decides to phone her grandmother and pretend that she used to work with her birth mother. She hopes to get a contact address for her birth mother in this way. The grandmother passes her on to her mother's sister for the address. However, although the daughter tries to hide her true identity, both her grandmother and her aunt guess who she really is.

The Phone Call

I have had my grandmother's Highland number
for four months now burning a hole in my filofax.

Something this morning gives me courage
to close the kitchen door and dial.

My grandmother's voice sounds much younger
'I used to work ages ago with your daughter

Elizabeth, do you have her present address?'
Sorry, she says, *No, but one of the girls*

will have it. She gives me another Highland number
wishing me luck. *What did you say your name was?*

Thirty minutes later my mother's sister
asks lots of questions – *Where did you work?*

How long ago was that? What age are you?
Forty I lie. *For a minute I thought ...*

But if you're forty, you can't be.
I know she knows. The game's a bogey.

Actually I'm 26. *I thought so love.*
I thought it was you. Mam knew too.

She just rang to warn me you'd ring.
How are you? How's your life been?

I'll give her yours. She'll write.
I'm sure you understand. I do. I do.

What are you really thinking?

❶ Work in a group of three:
  ❏ One of you should take the role of the daughter
  ❏ One of you should take the role of the grandmother
  ❏ One of you should take the role of the aunt

❷ In role, improvise the following telephone conversations:
  ❏ The daughter speaking to her grandmother
  ❏ The daughter speaking to her aunt
  ❏ The grandmother speaking to the aunt

Every so often, pause or 'freeze' the telephone conversation so that each character can speak their 'inner' thoughts out loud. This technique is called 'thought tracking'. There is likely to be a difference between what each character is *saying* during the telephone conversation and what they are actually *thinking*!

❸ Present your thought tracking to another group or the rest of the class.

Solving problems

Dr Edward de Bono is famous for his teaching of thinking as a skill. He decided that the main problem with thinking is confusion: that we try to do too much at once. He says that 'Emotions, information, logic, hope and creativity all crowd in on us. It is like juggling too many balls at once'.

To help us make our thinking processes clearer, Edward de Bono developed what he calls the six thinking hats. Each hat allows a thinker to do one thing at a time. The six hats are:

The white hat: What are the facts? Be objective

The red hat: This gives you the opportunity to express your feelings

The black hat: This is the hat of caution – what are the dangers or problems?

The yellow hat: This is the sunshine hat. Be positive and optimistic!

The green hat: Think of growth. This is the creative hat – improve ideas, suggest new ones

The blue hat: The cool hat. The person wearing this hat will lead the session by focusing the thinking, asking the right questions and summing up at the end

Wearing a hat

❶ You are going to work in groups of six to complete a 'thinking hat' activity related to the poem 'The Phone Call' by Jackie Kay. This will be your 'home' group. Decide who will 'wear' each hat in your group.

❷ Now re-group so that you are working with other pupils who have the same colour hat as you. Use your thinking hat to discuss the poem 'The Phone Call'. Respond to the poem in a manner appropriate to the hat you have. For example, if you are wearing a red hat, discuss the effect the poem had on your feelings. Once you have discussed your ideas, return to your 'home' group.

❸ Take it in turns to report back the thinking from your hat colour group. Note key points from your discussion. Report back in this order:

- ❏ **Blue hat:** Define the situation
- ❏ **White hat:** What are the facts?
- ❏ **Red hat:** Get the feelings out in the open
- ❏ **Yellow hat:** Be positive
- ❏ **Black hat:** What are the problems?
- ❏ **Green hat:** What new ideas or solutions do you have?
- ❏ **Blue hat:** Sum up

Use the talk toolkit below to help you cooperate and develop your ideas.

Cooperate and negotiate	**Echo and develop ideas**
Should we …?	So you think that …?
Would it be a good idea if …?	Does that mean …?
Do not use 'never' or 'always'	We could consider …

Express more complex views	**Choose your words carefully. There are many shades of meaning**
I don't like it but I can understand why …	The daughter was curious/
Although I wouldn't, I can see why some people would …	worried/anxious

In the hot seat!

Hot seating is a useful drama technique that helps you to probe and question. By hot seating a person or character you can develop a deeper understanding of their motives and attitudes. Imagine that you had the chance to put Jackie Kay in the hot seat and speak to her about her poetry. What sorts of questions would you like to ask her? Would you ask her, for example, about where the ideas for her poems come from or would you ask her about her style and techniques as a writer?

TASK

❶ In this part of the unit you will prepare to hot seat Jackie Kay in order to question her about her writing. To prepare for this, you will need to look back through your reading journal and note questions.

❷ When you have prepared your questions, in pairs take turns either assuming the role of Jackie Kay or asking her questions.

❸ Next, look back at the characters described in Jackie Kay's poems. Reflect on the questions that you would like to ask them. For example, how did the narrator in 'Duncan Gets Expelled' feel when the bullies were caught? Make notes to prepare for the hot seating session.

❹ Hot seat the different characters.

Writing about Jackie Kay's poems

As the final piece of work in this unit, you will write an essay comparing two poems of your choice by Jackie Kay. The title of your essay is:

'Compare at least two poems by Jackie Kay. Comment on how key ideas are developed and how the poet uses structure and language to express them'

You need to refer closely to your reading journal when making your choice of poems. This is a piece of critical writing where you will need to demonstrate that:

- You have understood the key ideas in the poems and how they have been developed
- You are a critical reader able to ask questions about a text
- You can comment on a writer's use of structure and style, and the effect these have on a reader

Key ingredients in the essay

You will need to discuss the ways that Jackie Kay uses techniques as a writer and the **effect** they have on the reader. You will also need to demonstrate that you have understood the subject matter, i.e. the main ideas and themes. You will need to comment on how key ideas and themes are developed. You will do this by:

1   Discussing the structure of the poems:
- Line length
- Use of statements, questions and exclamations
- Breaks in stanzas
2   Discussing the poet's use of language:
- Key words
- Dramatic vocabulary
- Powerful verbs
- Unusual use of words
- Imagery
- Patterns of language
- Dialogue
3   Saying something about the context in which the poem was written:
- Information on the poet's background and motives for writing
4   Discussing the effect on a reader:
- Personal response

A good essay will...

- Answer the question!

- Show knowledge of the poems

- Have a formal tone, e.g. 'The poet uses imagery to…'

- Use the present tense to discuss ideas, e.g. 'This suggests that…'

- Use the past tense to describe something that happened in the past, e.g. 'Jackie Kay was adopted'

- Use appropriate technical vocabulary, e.g. structure, tone, metaphor

- Use connectives of comparison or contrast, e.g. 'In comparison to…'

- Use simple sentences for clarity, e.g. 'The narrator of the poem is clearly unhappy and upset.'

- Use complex sentences for more detail, e.g. 'The use of short statements in the first stanza of the poem emphasises that the narrator is in no doubt about how they feel.'

- Support points made with evidence, e.g. 'The first line of the stanza, "I am totally stressed out", sums up the narrator's feelings.'

- Use quotations and integrate them into your writing, e.g. 'The word "stressed" is repeated throughout the poem to emphasise the narrator's desperation.'

UNIT 2 Phoney debate

In this unit you will learn about the following key objectives:

Prepositions and connectives – learning how to use a wider range of words which link sentences and ideas in your writing

Grouping sentences – exploring the ways different writers group sentences to show how their thoughts are developing in a logical sequence

Independent research – researching a topic using a variety of skills and sources

Balanced analysis – employing the skills that you have learned and practised in order to write your own balanced analysis of an issue

KEY OBJECTIVES

Do you or any of your friends own a mobile phone? Teenagers seem to love them; you can spend hours chatting to your friends or texting messages to each other. Many adults also find them invaluable, using them for business and social purposes. Many people, however, find them intrusive and irritating and would like to see them banned from public places. And what about the hidden cost of all those hours spent chatting to your friends? As with many issues, there are two sides to the debate about mobile phones. Love them or hate them? Either way, you are bound to have an opinion.

In this unit you are going to learn how to write a balanced analysis of the advantages and disadvantages of teenagers having mobile phones.

You will need to:

● Keep in mind the features of this style of writing
● Present the arguments from the differing viewpoints, giving equal weight to each
● Use quotations from acknowledged sources or experts
● Use logical connectives, e.g. in addition, therefore
● Use the present tense

Mindmapping – activating prior knowledge

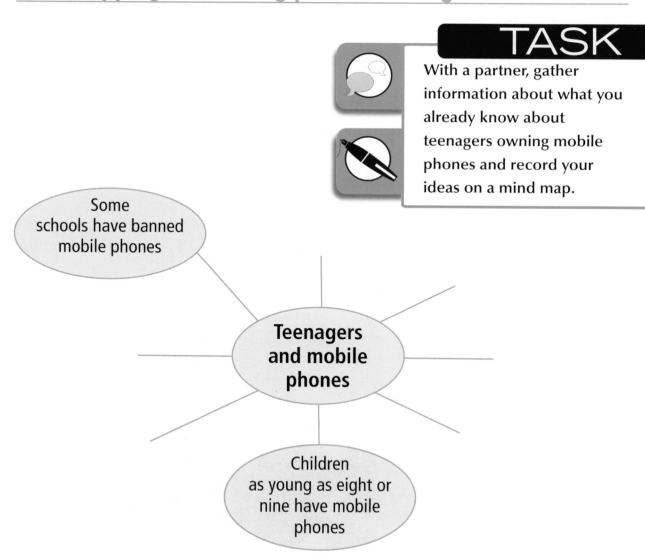

TASK

With a partner, gather information about what you already know about teenagers owning mobile phones and record your ideas on a mind map.

Some schools have banned mobile phones

Teenagers and mobile phones

Children as young as eight or nine have mobile phones

Asking questions

What more do you want to know? You should set yourself a number of questions to answer later. Write these in your exercise book or on paper.

You might think about mobile phones in relation to:

- Education
- Social issues
- Health
- Safety
- Crime

Here are a few ideas to get you started:

❑ Is it important for everyone to have access to technology?

❑ Is the world a safer place because of new technology?

❑

❑

❑

Remember: You are asking the questions, *not* answering them.

A research map

Work with a partner to complete a copy of the research map. You should transfer your questions into the appropriate boxes and then decide where you will look to find the answers.

Remember: You may use more than one source, for example, a newspaper article or a web page.

All sources need to be acknowledged. Keep a note of the writer, publication title and its date, for example Charles Shoebridge, *Guardian Unlimited*, 8 January 2002.

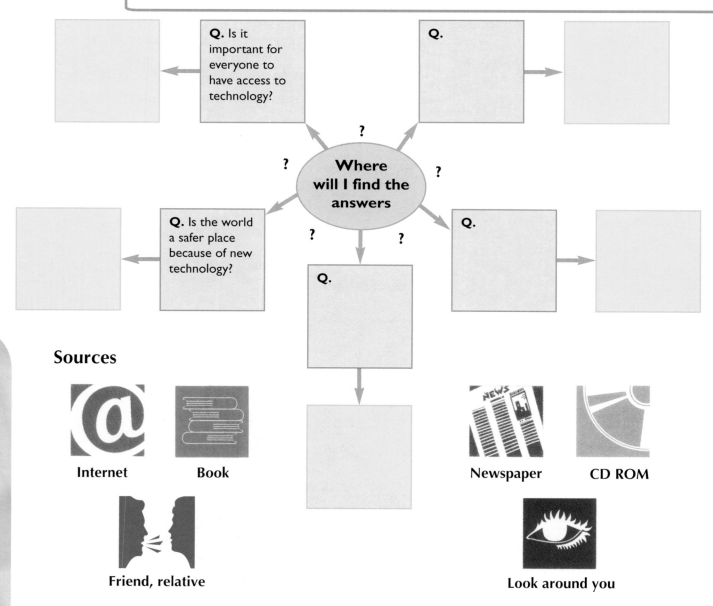

Q. Is it important for everyone to have access to technology?

Q.

Where will I find the answers

Q. Is the world a safer place because of new technology?

Q.

Q.

Sources

Internet

Book

Newspaper

CD ROM

Friend, relative

Look around you

A *Headline*

B *Picture with caption*

C *Lead paragraph*

D *Picture with sub-heading*

E *Bullet pointed list*

F *Quotation (statement) from interested party*

G *Hot links*

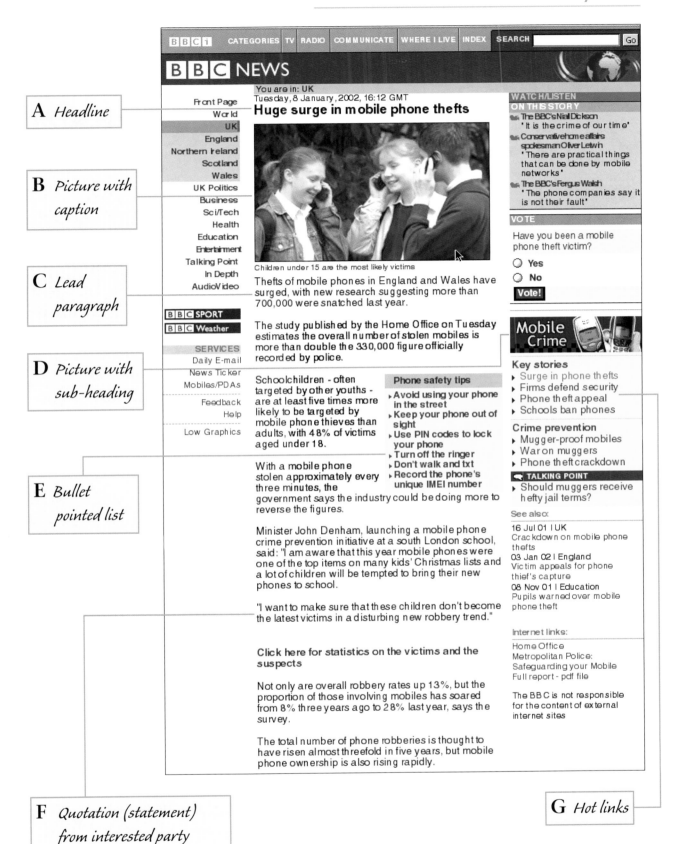

BBCi | CATEGORIES | TV | RADIO | COMMUNICATE | WHERE I LIVE | INDEX | SEARCH [   ] Go

BBC NEWS

Front Page
World
UK
England
Northern Ireland
Scotland
Wales
UK Politics
Business
Sci/Tech
Health
Education
Entertainment
Talking Point
In Depth
AudioVideo

BBC SPORT
BBC Weather

SERVICES
Daily E-mail
News Ticker
Mobiles/PDAs

Feedback
Help

Low Graphics

You are in: UK
Tuesday, 8 January, 2002, 16:12 GMT
Huge surge in mobile phone thefts

Children under 15 are the most likely victims

Thefts of mobile phones in England and Wales have surged, with new research suggesting more than 700,000 were snatched last year.

The study published by the Home Office on Tuesday estimates the overall number of stolen mobiles is more than double the 330,000 figure officially recorded by police.

Schoolchildren - often targeted by other youths - are at least five times more likely to be targeted by mobile phone thieves than adults, with 48% of victims aged under 18.

With a mobile phone stolen approximately every three minutes, the government says the industry could be doing more to reverse the figures.

Phone safety tips
- Avoid using your phone in the street
- Keep your phone out of sight
- Use PIN codes to lock your phone
- Turn off the ringer
- Don't walk and txt
- Record the phone's unique IMEI number

Minister John Denham, launching a mobile phone crime prevention initiative at a south London school, said: "I am aware that this year mobile phones were one of the top items on many kids' Christmas lists and a lot of children will be tempted to bring their new phones to school.

"I want to make sure that these children don't become the latest victims in a disturbing new robbery trend."

Click here for statistics on the victims and the suspects

Not only are overall robbery rates up 13%, but the proportion of those involving mobiles has soared from 8% three years ago to 28% last year, says the survey.

The total number of phone robberies is thought to have risen almost threefold in five years, but mobile phone ownership is also rising rapidly.

WATCH/LISTEN
ON THIS STORY
- The BBC's Niall Dickson 'It is the crime of our time'
- Conservative home affairs spokesman Oliver Letwin 'There are practical things that can be done by mobile networks'
- The BBC's Fergus Walsh 'The phone companies say it is not their fault'

VOTE
Have you been a mobile phone theft victim?
○ Yes
○ No
Vote!

Mobile Crime

Key stories
▸ Surge in phone thefts
▸ Firms defend security
▸ Phone theft appeal
▸ Schools ban phones

Crime prevention
▸ Mugger-proof mobiles
▸ War on muggers
▸ Phone theft crackdown

TALKING POINT
▸ Should muggers receive hefty jail terms?

See also:

16 Jul 01 | UK
Crackdown on mobile phone thefts
03 Jan 02 | England
Victim appeals for phone thief's capture
08 Nov 01 | Education
Pupils warned over mobile phone theft

Internet links:

Home Office
Metropolitan Police:
Safeguarding your Mobile
Full report - pdf file

The BBC is not responsible for the content of external internet sites

Skimming and scanning

Skimming is reading for general knowledge of a text. **Scanning** is reading for specific information.

You are going to skim the web page on page 33. You will need to consider the following:

❶ Where will you look first for information?

❷ What type of information are you looking for?

❸ How can the annotations help you?

❹ List the letters in a sequence to prioritise their importance. Start with the source that gives the most information. Next to each letter make a note of what you learn from this section.

For example, if you think the section labelled **A** gives you the most information, write **A** at the top of your list. Next to it, briefly make a note of what this section tells you.

---

1   **A**: Headline – states what the article is about – an increase in mobile phone thefts.

2

Next you need to scan the text to find the answers to the following questions. Share your responses with a partner.

❶ How many mobile phones were snatched last year?

❷ How many victims are under 18 years of age?

❸ What is the top item on many teenagers' Christmas list, according to minister John Denham?

TASK

① Read the extracts A, B, C, D, E and F.

② Copy the table and make a note under the relevant heading of what each extract tells you about the advantages or disadvantages of mobile phones.

Paragraph	Advantages	Disadvantages
A		
B		
C		
D		
E		
F		

Points of view

The panel

The question: At least one in 20 teenagers was robbed of a mobile phone last year. Would children be better off without them?

A
Mary Crowley,
Spokeswoman, Parenting,
Education and Support Forum
There is hugh commercial pressure on children to own mobile phones and this pressure is transferred to their parents. Of course, it's great to be able to phone them and say, "Where are you?" If someone demands a phone, they should hand it over – it's not worth losing your life over. We must think carefully about advising children how to use mobile phones, but we should allow teenagers to have them.

B
Alexander
Dowty, 13 year-old
member of Children's Express
news agency
The girl who was shot in the head for her phone lives just around the corner from me. I don't wander around my area anymore because I don't really think it's safe. I do have a mobile phone and I haven't been mugged for it. I wouldn't get rid of it. My mum likes me to have one so she can keep in contact with me when I'm out.

C
Tim Godwin, Deputy assistant commissioner of the Metropolitan police

It is appropriate for parents to buy teenagers mobile phones, but they do have a responsibility to give some advice about their use, because owning a mobile phone puts their son or daughter at risk of becoming a victim of street crime. To a street robber, a phone is perceived as cash, so phones should be handled the way you would handle cash in the street.

D
Jacqui Brookes, Chief executive, Federation of Communication Services

You should look after your mobile phone like any valuable possession. Security-mark the phone with your postcode and street number, keep a note of your phone's serial number, and inform the police if it is stolen. Above all, be aware of your surroundings and use your phone carefully and discreetly.

E
Lee Jasper, Adviser to the Mayor of London on race and policing

Instead of buying teenagers expensive mobile phones, some might be better off with pagers. The present debate about mobile phone theft from young people is focusing on race and crime when it should actually be focusing on poverty, social exclusion and crime.

F
Mary MacLeod, Chief executive, National Family and Parenting Institute

Parents are caught between a rock and a hard place with mobile phones. They are a great source of comfort and security, because they allow parents to find out where their children are and keep in touch with them. At the same time, they make young people targets for crime.

Interviews by Diane Taylor

TASK

Read the introduction from the book *TXT TLK*.

With a partner, discuss the annotations and suggest how language is being used to persuade the reader that a mobile phone is a necessity for a teenager.

TXT TLK

Introduction

If you're the owner of a mobile phone, you're not alone. Millions of people across the world are mobile mad — nearly 40 million people in Britain alone. Chances are your teachers have one, the 'rents, even your grandparents have a mobile. If you don't own one, get with the programme girl. Maybe you're worried it'll cost stacks of cash (it won't) or you think you don't need one. Well trust me, by the end of this book you will!

Mobiles are fun, a cool way of staying in touch and can even reflect what kind of chick you are. They're especially important for us girl-shapes cos everyone knows how much we love to gossip! But the best thing is, as soon as you've got a mobile, you can take part in the biggest and coolest craze around, texting. how did we ever live without it? To be a top texter, you gotta speak the lingo, and if you don't know it, this book will tell you. If you reckon you're a top texter, this book is full of stories from other text mad gels as well as stuff about customising your phone and web reviews.

So, if you've got a phone, have it within dialling distance while you're reading this book. You'll find out loads of stuff you never knew. If you haven't got a mobile, this book will tell you how to buy one, what the jiggins all this texting business is about and give you a sneaky peek at the phones of the future. Either way, you're one lucky girl cos in your hands is the ultimate girls' guide to texting, icons and all things mobile. So if you've got a signal . . . let's get dialling s

Chantelle Horton

Key of techniques used to persuade

〜〜 Addressing people directly	est Superlatives
– – Alliteration	▨ Flattery and emotive language
⬯ Hyperbole (exaggeration)	t Technical language
✦ Colloquial (appropriate language for audience)	1 2 Pattern of three 3
! Punctuation	| Counter-argument
? Rhetorical question (a question that doesn't need an answer)	s Slogan (summarising message)

❶ Read the following editorial from the *Mirror*. A key has been provided of some of the language features sometimes used in editorials.

❷ Annotate a copy of the editorial to evaluate the information it provides.

❸ How does the writer use these language features to persuade the reader of his opinion?

Mirror.co.uk

A phoney call for longer sentences

Paul Crozier, Bristol, 1 February 2002, the *Mirror*

HAVEN'T the government and the Law Lords learned anything from knee-jerk reactions?

The Lord Chief Justice, Lord Woolf, has increased sentences for mobile-phone muggers to five years, with a minimum of 18 months (The *Mirror*, January 31).

While we all abhor phone theft and agree it's on the increase and becoming increasingly violent, what we really need is a proper scale of sentencing.

There are convicted rapists and murderers who are getting less prison time than someone who threatened to use a knife to steal a mobile. Isn't it time the criminal justice system was overhauled?

Sentencing has to be consistent nationwide and judges should be given specific guidlines to follow.

TASK

❶ Read the newspaper article on page 40 which is from the *Guardian* newspaper.

❷ Work with a partner to annotate or text mark examples of the following features on a copy of the text:

❏ The main topic of the article (look at the headline and introductory paragraph)

❏ The topic sentence of each paragraph

❏ Supporting statements

❏ Opposing statements

❏ Reference to research

❏ Use of connectives

❏ Formal **register**

Register: the language used to create a particular style or tone

Mobile muggings highlight a wider problem

The real concern is why society is incapable of dealing with juvenile crime, writes Charles Shoebridge

Metropolitan Police claims last week, that soaring robbers could be blamed on the need for increased security patrols since September 11, do not stand scrutiny.

Although offences more than doubled in the year to December 2001, the figures are consistent with a long-established increase in this type of crime.

In the first six months of 2001, street robberies in the capital rose by over 20%, to some 5,500 offences in July. The average monthly figure of 6,400 after the US attacks shows therefore a similar rate of increase.

Claims that robbery has been fuelled by mobile phone ownership are more justified, with more than 28% of offences now involving a mobile phone. This, however, does not in itself explain why robberies are increasing.

According to the Home Office, street robberies have increased nationally by 13% over the last two years. Had robberies where only phones were stolen been excluded, the figure would have been 8%. The increase in street robbery cannot, therefore, be blamed entirely on mobile phones.

It is not enough to say that poverty alone is a reason for such criminality. The boys who steal do not, generally, have any more materially difficult lives than those on the same estates who do not. Experience suggests, however, that many are excluded from school, and even more are missing a positive male role model.

In resolving street robbery, there are factors at work beyond the ability of the police alone to control. The issue is complex, and separate from that of mobile phones. It involves uncomfortable truths of victimised society in terms of both victim and perpetrator.

Regardless of those complexities, the inexorable rise of street robbery marks the apparent inability of society and, in particular, the criminal justice system, to adequately deal with juvenile violent crime. This, rather than the technical properties of phones, is the key issue to be addressed.

Charles Shoebridge was a serving Metropolitan police officer from 1988 to 2000.

The *Guardian*, 8 January 2002

TASK

❶ Re-read the final paragraph of Charles Shoebridge's 'Mobile muggings' article.

❷ With your partner, discuss your responses to the following questions:
- ❏ What point does Shoebridge make in his conclusion?
- ❏ How does this paragraph link back to the first paragraph of the article?

TASK

❶ The extract below from *TXT TLK* has an intended audience of young people. It uses an informal register and non-standard features of English. Can you spot them? Make a note of them.

❷ Rewrite the *TXT TLK* extract with your teacher as the new intended audience. Use a formal register and Standard English throughout.

You may like to consider:
- ❏ The vocabulary
- ❏ The grammar
- ❏ The punctuation

TXT TLK

The massive popularity of texting ain't anything to do with old crinklies – Oh no! Most text messages are sent by us kids and the most popular time to text is Friday night. Must be all those end of schoolweek hissy fits! So why is texting so popular?

Chantelle Horton

Read the following essay which weighs up both sides of an argument. The argument concerns homework. Is homework useful? Does it provide pupils with a valuable opportunity to extend their learning and to work independently? Or does it put too much unnecessary pressure on pupils, parents and teachers alike? As we discovered early on in this unit, there are two sides to most issues.

Is it necessary to set homework?

There is a lot of discussion about whether the setting of homework is beneficial. Whilst many people believe that completing homework is a valuable task, which reinforces and extends work carried out in school, others believe that it is an unnecessary burden, wasting time that could be better spent pursuing interests and activities not catered for in the school curriculum.

Firstly, homework proponents argue that time spent on homework is an invaluable opportunity to practise skills and vital independent research techniques, the very skills which are necessary to further academic study and the world of work.

In addition, government figures show that those 37 per cent of students who regularly spend time on homework achieve greater academic success and have fewer opportunities to get into trouble.

However, although there are undoubtedly strong arguments in favour of regular homework, there are many who see this as an erosion of free time that could have been used perfecting skills and talents not included in the present academic curriculum. While it is true that students in Britain have the opportunity to specialise to a significant degree, it could also be argued that being required to spend further time on the academic curriculum at home leaves no time to develop personal interests, to engage in a broad range of clubs and activities, or to pursue one particular talent, for example learning how to play a musical instrument.

Moreover, there is, at present, great concern about the levels of obesity in young people. Restricting opportunities to engage in a more active lifestyle by the regular setting of homework can only increase the potential for obesity with dire consequences for the future health of the nation. It is widely reported that in ten years' time at least 40 per cent of the population will be clinically obese.

In conclusion, although it can be argued that there are benefits in reinforcing what you have already learned and developing independent study skills, too much time spent on homework can restrict the pursuit of other hobbies and talents and the opportunities available to physical well-being.

Now match the essay to the following table to see how a balanced analysis, which weighs up two sides of an argument, can be structured.

Writing a balanced argument	
Introduction	• Introduces the issue • Briefly explains why the issue is so important • Briefly explains that there is a difference of opinion about the issue
Arguments for the case	• Supporting arguments using exemplification and appropriate connective
Further arguments for the case	• Supporting evidence introduced by a connective that shows information is being added
Arguments against the case	• Opposing opinion using connective that indicates reservation
Further arguments against the case	• Further examples to strengthen the opposing case introduced by an appropriate connective
Conclusion	• Restates the issue • Presents one or two sentences which summarise the arguments in favour of the case • Presents one or two sentences which summarise reservations about the case • Final sentence to conclude the essay

On page 30, you were told that you would be learning how to write a balanced analysis of the advantages and disadvantages of teenagers having mobile phones.

TASK

Draft your essay: Should teenagers have mobile phones?

The following sentence starters may help you to structure your balanced argument:
- There is a lot of discussion about…
- Firstly…
- Furthermore…
- In addition…
- On the other hand…
- However…
- Despite…
- In conclusion…

Remember: Your final written balanced analysis should:
- Use Standard English
- Use a formal register
- Be appropriate for your intended audience
- Use quotations from acknowledged sources or experts
- Use logical connectives, e.g. in addition, therefore
- Use the present tense
- Present the arguments from the differing viewpoints, giving equal weight to each.

Editing your work

When you have completed your draft, use these checklists to improve your writing. Work with a partner.

❶ Look at your drafting and editing. Have you:
- ❏ Written a suitable opening paragraph?
- ❏ Presented both sides of the argument?
- ❏ Written in the present tense?
- ❏ Used a formal register?
- ❏ Used appropriate connectives?
- ❏ Written a concluding paragraph?
- ❏ Varied your sentence construction?
- ❏ Acknowledged your sources?

Make any changes.

❷ Look at the accuracy of your writing. Have you:
- ❏ Punctuated your sentences correctly, including semi-colons and commas to mark boundaries within complex sentences?
- ❏ Checked your spellings?
- ❏ Used question marks for rhetorical questions?
- ❏ Divided your writing into paragraphs?

Make your corrections.

❸ Ask your teacher if you need more help. Remember to proofread the final copy of your balanced analysis before submitting it for assessment.

Reviewing your work

Before your teacher has commented on your work, ask yourself the following questions:

- What have I learned about carrying out independent research?

- What have I learned about writing a balanced argument?

- What do I think that I have done well? Give reasons.

- If I could complete the task again, what would I do differently? Give reasons.

- How do I think I could use what I have learned in the future?

TASK

You might like to practise your skills and extend yourself further by writing a balanced analysis of one of the following:

❶ What are the advantages and disadvantages of the internet?

❷ What are the advantages and disadvantages of testing cosmetics and medicines on animals?

UNIT 3 *Holes* by Louis Sachar

In this unit you will learn about the following key objectives:

Interpret a text – learning how to be a critical reader who asks questions and reflects upon the writer's choice of particular styles and techniques. This involves finding out how readers interact with a text to gain its full meaning. You will learn not only **what** you are reading but **how** you are reading it

Trace developments – tracing how the writer develops themes, values and ideas in a text. This involves using a range of reading strategies, which you will be able to use again when you read other novels. You will also learn how to record and present the evidence you have collected about the text

In this unit you will investigate Louis Sachar's powerful novel *Holes*. This is an exciting and thought-provoking novel that explores ideas of friendship, imprisonment and the impact of the past on the present.

TASK

❶ Your first impression of a novel is often a very important one. Look at these two front covers.

❷ What do they tell you about the novel and what do they lead you to expect?

❸ Which design appeals to you most and why?

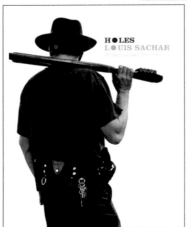

Holes by Louis Sachar, Bloomsbury.

Chapters 1–2

TASK

Read the opening section of the novel, making a note of any interesting features. Then read the extract below, noticing how some of those features have been annotated by a reader.

Present tense locates the story in the reader's own time

People shriveled as well as lake. Powerful image of death

Short blunt sentences, meant to jolt the reader into interest and attention. Facts give story a non-fiction feel

Creates a barren atmosphere – prepares the reader for the atmosphere at the camp. Contrast between past and present introduced

Barren atmosphere further reinforced

Hardly any vegetation – shows the extreme heat

Author expresses irony

More facts about the extreme environment to show the reader how harsh the conditions are

Sense of physical danger. Direct address to the reader – almost a conversational tone

So there is some life and comfort there?

Whose?

Good tactic by author – sets up idea then contradicts it

There is no lake at Camp Green Lake. There once was a very large lake here, the largest lake in Texas. That was over a hundred years ago. Now it is just a dry, flat wasteland. There used to be a town of Green Lake as well. The town shriveled and dried up along with the lake, and the people who lived there. During the summer the daytime temperature hovers around ninety-five degrees in the shade – if you can find any shade. There's not much shade in a big dry lake. The only trees are two old oaks on the eastern edge of the 'lake.' A hammock is stretched between the two trees, and a log cabin stands behind that. The campers are forbidden to lie in the hammock. It belongs to the Warden. The Warden owns the shade.

If this is a prison ('Warden') then why are the prisoners called 'campers'? Again the reader's interest is engaged

Who are the campers and who is the Warden? The reader is intrigued. The Warden already seems powerful. Note the capital W

As you read on, notice how the writer has constructed his first chapter so that the reader is immediately drawn into the story. The opening chapter of a novel is often full of un-answered questions in order to engage the interest of the reader

TASK

❶ What are the unanswered questions in the first two chapters of *Holes*? What questions spring into the reader's mind?

❷ In pairs, write down five questions you would like answered. Record your questions as a whole class on a large sheet of paper and keep them for later.

Meet Stanley Yelnats – the unluckiest boy on earth

Chapters 3–4

Stanley Yelnats is the main character in *Holes*. Look carefully at the way Louis Sachar introduces Stanley in these chapters. The writer has carefully constructed Stanley's character in these early chapters, with the intention of developing him as events unfold.

We learn about characters through:

● What they say
● What they look like
● Their circumstances
● Their thoughts and feelings
● What others say about them

TASK

Read the descriptions on page 50 of three characters from the novel.

❶ Look at the sentences which have been underlined in each extract.
❷ What can you infer about each character from this description?

English Works

A man was sitting with his feet up on a desk. He turned his head when Stanley and the guard entered, but otherwise didn't move. Even though he was inside, he wore sunglasses and a cowboy hat. He also held a can of soda, and the sight of it made Stanley even more aware of his own thirst.

Mr. Pendanski was younger than Mr. Sir, and not nearly as scary looking. The top of his head was shaved so close it was almost bald, but his face was covered in a thick curly black beard. His nose was badly sunburned.

'Zigzag had to be the 'weirdest dude' Stanley had ever seen. He had a long skinny neck, and a big round head with wild frizzy blond hair that stuck out in all directions. His head seemed to bob up and down on his neck, like it was on a spring.'

TASK

Although Stanley is the main character in the novel, he does not seem to be a typical hero.

❶ Use a copy of the following table to record information about how Louis Sachar presents Stanley in Chapter 3. You should focus on his appearance and his family background as well as his character.

❷ For each point, provide evidence in the form of a quotation which may be taken from the dialogue or from the narrative. The grid has been started for you.

Key point	Textual evidence
He is overweight	'Stanley weighed three times as much as the other boy'

You will be able to add to the grid as Stanley develops and changes in the novel. This will help you to compare his character at different points in the story.

Weaving the story

Chapters 5–7

In Chapter 7 of *Holes* Louis Sachar takes his reader back in time. He tells the story of Elya Yelnats, Stanley's great, great grandfather, and his experiences with Myra and Madame Zeroni. The writer here has made an interesting **narrative** choice. He takes the reader back in time in the form of a **flashback** and introduces a number of new characters. The writer has created two plots or storylines which are **juxtaposed**. Once again the reader is invited to ask questions. Will the two plots meet at any point?

> **g** **Flashback:** when the story suddenly jumps back in time. It can often give essential background to the story and characters
>
> **Juxtaposition:** when two ideas are placed side by side, for effect
>
> **Multiple narratives:** stories which are told from more than one point of view
>
> **Narrative structure:** a writer may decide to structure a story in a particular way, for example through the use of a flashback
>
> **Narrative voice:** the point of view from which a story is told. Some stories are told in the first person, from the point of view of a character in the story; others employ a third person, omniscient (all knowing) narrator

GLOSSARY

It can be helpful to sketch out the different plot lines, particularly when there are several. This can also help us to remember and explain complex storylines later.

TASK

In pairs, study the sketch overleaf of the two plots and answer the questions below.

❶ Why has Louis Sachar chosen to place these two very different stories alongside each other?

❷ How does one story relate to the other?

❸ When you read about Stanley's pain as he is trying to dig his first hole, do you make any connections with Elya's story? What could these connections be?

❹ What has your investigation revealed to you about Louis Sachar's narrative technique?

Two plots

**Stanley begins
first hole** → **Finds it easier as he
goes deeper**

Elya asks to marry Myra/carries pig

Elya doesn't follow instructions

Stanley's blisters rip open

The pigs weigh the same!

**Stanley climbs out and
starts again**

**Stanley continues to
dig and suffer**

Elya rejects Myra

Elya breaks his promise

Digging into themes – imprisonment

Chapters
8–10

You are now going to think about how writers develop themes and ideas in their writing. One of the main themes in *Holes* is imprisonment. The reader is shown how Stanley and the other boys in the camp try to cope with the very difficult life they have there.

At the end of Chapter 4, Mr. Sir says, 'Nobody runs away from here. We don't need a fence. Know why? Because we've got the only water for a hundred miles. You want to run away? You'll be buzzard food in three days.' One of the main difficulties that Stanley has to cope with is that he loses almost all of his privacy and personal freedom.

You can use Post-it notes to plot how a theme develops in a novel. For example, you could analyse Mr. Sir's words in the following way:

TASK

In a pair, take three minutes to write down as many facts as you can about life at Camp Green Lake. Focus on the hardships that the boys have to endure. Share your ideas with the rest of the class.

Stanley's imprisonment is unusual.

There are no walls or fences, but the scorching desert around him is his boundary.

This is particularly <u>cruel</u> because the camp looks as though it is a place of ~~freedom~~, but the boys cannot escape.

The note is brief and refers directly to the quotation

The reader reflects upon the meaning of the quotation chosen

The main theme is linked to cruelty and this can be traced in again later. The reader underlines this as important

TASK

Work with a partner to produce five more Post-its which trace the development of the theme of imprisonment in this part of the novel.

Meet the Warden

Chapters 11–14

TASK

Think back to the first few chapters of the novel. What kind of character did you expect the Warden to be?

Louis Sachar deliberately leads the reader astray in his presentation of the Warden. Many readers will have assumed that the Warden was a man. However, the Warden in *Holes* turns out to be a very interesting woman. If you look back through the novel, you will find that no references to the Warden's gender were ever made. If you inferred, like many readers, that the Warden was a man, you were using a reading strategy. You were calling on your cultural and social experiences to help you to make sense of a text. It would be natural to assume that the warden of a boys' reform school would be a man, because many are.

TASK

As you read the extract on page 55, make a note of the way the writer introduces the character of the Warden. Look back at your earlier work on Stanley to remind yourself of how a writer can present a character.

A tall woman with red hair stepped out of the passenger side. She looked even taller than she was, since Stanley was down in his hole. She wore a black cowboy hat and black cowboy boots which were studded with turquoise stones. The sleeves on her shirt were rolled up, and her arms were covered with freckles, as was her face. She walked right up to X-Ray …

… "Your work will be rewarded." She turned to Mr. Pendanski. "Drive X-Ray back to camp. Let him take a double shower, and give him some clean clothes. But first I want you to fill everyone's canteen."

"I just filled them a little while ago," said Mr. Pendanski.

The Warden stared hard at him. "Excuse me" she said.
Her voice was soft.

"I had just filled them when Rex –"

"Excuse me,' the Warden said again. "Did I ask you when you last filled them?"

"No, but it's just –"

"Excuse me."

Mr. Pendanski stopped talking. The Warden wiggled her finger for him to come to her.

"It's hot and it's only going to get hotter," she said. "Now, these fine boys have been working hard. Don't you think it might be possible that they might have taken a drink since you filled their canteens?"

Mr. Pendanski said nothing …

…"May I see your canteen please."

Stanley handed it to her. Her fingernails were painted dark red.

She gently shook the canteen, letting the water swish inside the plastic container.

"Do you hear empty space?" she asked.

"Yes," said Mr. Pendanski.

"Then fill it," she said. "And the next time I tell you to do something, I expect you to do it without questioning my authority. If it's too much trouble for you to fill a canteen, I'll give you a shovel. You can dig the hole, and the Caveman can fill your canteen." She turned back to Stanley. "I don't think that would be too much trouble for you, would it?"

"No," said Stanley.

"So what will it be?" she asked Mr. Pendanski. "Do you want to fill the canteens or do you want to dig?"

"I'll fill the canteens," said Mr. Pendanski.

"Thank you."

A letter home Chapters 15–18

Read the letter from Stanley's mother below from Chapter 16.

Dear Stanley

It was wonderful to hear from you. Your letter made me feel like one of the other moms who can afford to send their kids to summer camp. I know it's not the same, but I am very proud of you for trying to make the best of a bad situation. Who knows! Maybe something good will come of this.

Your father thinks he is real close to a breakthrough on his sneaker project. I hope so. The landlord is threatening to evict us because of the odor.

I feel sorry for the little old lady who lived in a shoe. It must have smelled awful.

Love from both of us

❶ Think of three reasons why the writer has chosen to include the letter at this point. The following prompts might help you:
   ❏ What does it reveal about Stanley's parents?
   ❏ What effect does it have on the reader?
❷ Now read Stanley's reply below from Chapter 18.

Dear Mom and Dad

Camp is hard, but challenging. We've been running obstacle courses, and have to swim long distances on the lake. Tomorrow we learn to rock climb. I know that sounds scary, but don't worry, I'll be careful. It's not all fun and games here, but I think I'm getting a lot out of it. It builds character.

Why do you think Stanley chooses to create such a false impression of the camp?

The relationships which develop at Camp Green Lake are complex, and many of them depend on power. Look back at the extract which introduced the Warden. What do you learn about the relationship between Mr. Pendanski and the Warden?

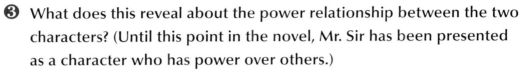

TASK

❶ Read Chapter 20 in which the Warden intimidates both Stanley and Mr. Sir. Focus on her behaviour towards Mr. Sir.

❷ What does she do to him and why?

❸ What does this reveal about the power relationship between the two characters? (Until this point in the novel, Mr. Sir has been presented as a character who has power over others.)

❹ How does this episode invite the reader to re-evaluate his or her response towards both Mr. Sir and the Warden?

TASK

Work in groups to explore Stanley's relationship with the following characters:

● Mr. Pendanski
● Zero
● Mr. Sir
● X Ray
● The Warden
● Zigzag

❶ Begin by looking for the moment in the novel when the two characters first meet. What are their first impressions of each other?

❷ Next, try to find two or three key moments when you discover something telling, for example, in Chapter 18 when Zigzag hits Stanley round the head with his shovel or in Chapter 11 when Stanley agrees to give X Ray his finds.

❸ Finally, search for moments when a relationship seems to develop or change in some way.

You may wish to use Post-it notes to record your notes or you may prefer to set your ideas out in the form of a flow chart.

Digging into the past

In Chapters 23, 25 and 26, Louis Sachar once again uses the narrative technique of a flashback. Sachar takes the reader back 110 years to tell the story of Kissin' Kate Barlow. Chapter 24 is sandwiched between these three chapters and tells of the brutality of life at the camp, as Mr. Sir continues to bully Stanley. Juxtaposed on either side of Chapter 24 is the story of Miss Katherine Barlow and her love for Sam. The townspeople murder Sam, and Kate becomes an outlaw. Both storylines are quite violent and shocking. Once again the writer has decided to juxtapose these two stories, so that Stanley's present can be compared to Kate's past life.

Cruelty is again shown in the novel and you will notice that Sam and Katherine were no freer in their lives than Stanley is at the camp. When reading a text such as this, it can be helpful to draw a table making comparisons between two plot lines. Often, the writer wants you to make a connection between past and present events.

TASK

Some of the table below is filled in for you. Make a copy of the grid and complete it, adding your own ideas.

Making Comparisons	
Stanley's time	**Kate's time**
Green Lake is…	Green Lake is…
The villain is…	

Mind the language!

Writers make a conscious decision to choose the kind of language that is suitable to the atmosphere they wish to create.

The language used will also make readers empathise with certain characters.

❶ Read the following extract closely. How has Sachar changed the style of his language in this part of the novel?

❷ How do you think he wants the reader to respond to the characters of Katherine and Sam?

She sat at her desk one afternoon, listening to the **pitter-patter** of the rain on the roof. **No water leaked into the classroom, except for the few drops that came from her eyes**.

"Onions! Hot **sweet** onions!" Sam called, out on the street.

She **ran to him**. She wanted to **throw her arms around him** but couldn't bring herself to do it. Instead she **hugged** Mary Lou's neck.

"Is something wrong?" he asked her.

"**Oh Sam**," she said. "**My heart is breaking**."

"**I can fix that**," said Sam.

She turned to him.

He **took hold of both of her hands**, and **kissed her**.

Because of the rain, there was nobody else out on the street. Even if there was, Katherine and Sam wouldn't have noticed. They were **lost in their own world**.

At that moment, however, Hattie Parker stepped out of the general store. They didn't see her, but she saw them. She pointed her quivering finger in their direction and whispered, "God will punish you!"

❶ What do you notice about the words and phrases in bold?

❷ Look at the final paragraph. How does Sachar introduce a change in atmosphere here?

❸ In pairs, take a few minutes to think about the following questions:
- ❑ From what you have read of the novel so far, how might the two plots converge?
- ❑ Why might this be the outcome?

❹ Share your ideas with the rest of the class.

Analysing the language

① Choose six of the words or phrases in bold from the extract on page 59. Comment on what those words and phrases add to the meaning of the text. Copy the table below and use it to record your ideas. One example has been done for you.

Quotation	Notes
'No water leaked into the classroom, except for the few drops that came from her eyes'.	Here Sachar cleverly reminds us of Sam, even though he is not present. He fixed the roof but the irony is that Katherine now has no reason to see him and so tears fall from her eyes.

Part Two – The last hole

What are your expectations of Part Two of the novel?

- It might be set in a different place?
- One of the characters might change a great deal?
- It might deal with a different time?
- The storylines might be very different?
- The themes might be different?
- The narrative style and language might be different?

At the beginning of Chapter 29, Louis Sachar develops a mini-climax. Notice how he does this. Below is the annotated opening of the chapter:

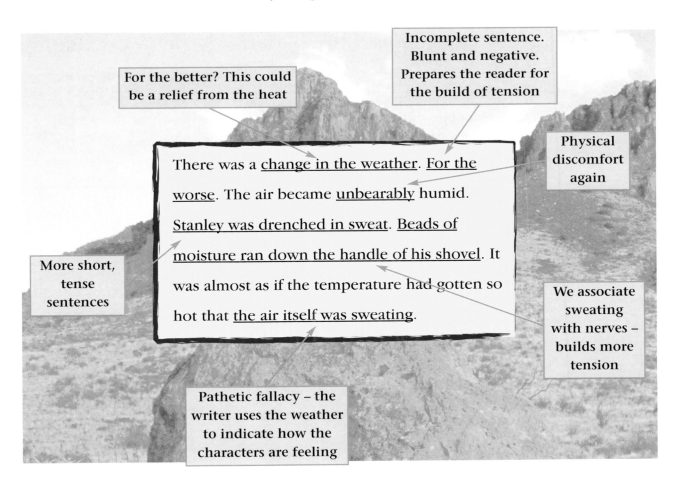

For the better? This could be a relief from the heat

Incomplete sentence. Blunt and negative. Prepares the reader for the build of tension

Physical discomfort again

There was a <u>change in the weather</u>. <u>For the worse</u>. The air became <u>unbearably</u> humid. <u>Stanley was drenched in sweat</u>. <u>Beads of moisture ran down the handle of his shovel</u>. It was almost as if the temperature had gotten so hot that <u>the air itself was sweating</u>.

More short, tense sentences

We associate sweating with nerves – builds more tension

Pathetic fallacy – the writer uses the weather to indicate how the characters are feeling

One of the most powerful ways for a writer to build to a climax is to gradually build up the tension.

TASK

Take two minutes to discuss with a partner three ways in which tension is created in the extract on page 61. Use the following prompts to help you to express your ideas:

- This example creates tension because…
- This would make the reader imagine…
- This would shock the reader because…
- The word… is powerful because…
- The tension is gradually built in this paragraph when…

Chapters 29–32 are full of tension as both Zero and Stanley make their escape.

TASK

Complete a copy of the spider diagram below to show how the writer creates tension in the novel. You do not need to restrict yourself to these four chapters.

Introducing tense and clipped dialogue, e.g. 'Quit pushing!… Lay off! …' (Zero and Armpit)

Appealing to the senses (touch, smell, taste, sight and sound), e.g. 'She ran her sharp wet nails very gently down his cheek. He felt his skin tingle.'

Writers create tension by …

Another prison visit

At this stage in your reading, you should update your earlier Post-it notes on the theme of imprisonment, which is often associated with lack of privacy, personal freedom and cruelty in the novel. You could use Post-it notes or, if you prefer, you could use another spider diagram.

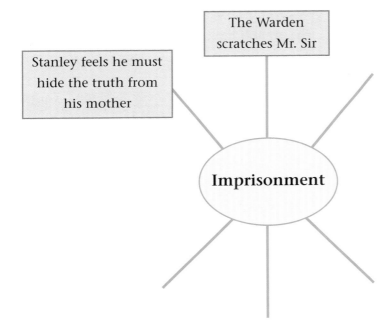

Clues and coincidences

Writers place clues throughout their novels for perceptive readers to find. A reader has to operate as a detective, searching for hints and clues throughout a text. Novels are not real life! Unlike real life, a text has been constructed by the writer, so everything in it has significance.

TASK

Read Chapters 34–36 in which Stanley sets out to find Zero. What do you think has significance in these chapters?

● Big Thumb?
● The Mary Lou?
● The peach flavoured 'sploosh'?

Real friends? Chapters 37–39

Earlier in this unit you started to track relationships between Stanley and some of the other characters at Camp Green Lake. It is now time to update your notes on his relationship with Zero. You will find that he and Zero have developed as characters as the plot has unfolded. Initially, it seemed as though their relationship was little more than a business transaction: Stanley taught Zero to read and, in return, Zero dug Stanley's holes. Now, however, it seems as though a deeper friendship is developing.

TASK

Look right back to Chapter 18 when Stanley refused to teach Zero to read.

Notice how you can structure your response:
- You make a point
- You support the point with textual evidence
- You elaborate a little further

For example:
- Stanley tells Zero he does not want to teach him to read because he is too tired
- 'His heart had hardened as well'
- This shows that life at the camp has changed Stanley

❶ Work in pairs to track the changing relationship between Stanley and Zero.
❷ Find five or six key moments in their relationship.
❸ Find textual evidence to support each one.
❹ Structure each three-part response like the example above.
❺ Develop each three-part response into a paragraph.
❻ Share your paragraphs with the class.

Empathising with the characters

Even though we know that Stanley and Zero are simply fictional characters created by the writer, it is possible, as readers, to become quite closely involved in their fate. It is known as **empathy** when the reader is able to 'step into the shoes' of a character and imaginatively experience his or her situation for themselves.

Imagine that Stanley can write to his mother at this point in the novel. Remember that he created a very false impression of life at Camp Green Lake in his earlier letter. What would he tell her about his experiences? Would he leave anything out? We know that he is anxious about his family and concerned that they will not know where he is.

TASK

Complete a copy of the letter below. Try and include details of:

- Stanley's relationship with Zero
- Life at the camp
- The Warden and Mr. Sir
- The other boys

- The reasons why Stanley and Zero ran away
- Stanley's feelings
- Stanley's style of speaking

Dear Mom,

Just thought that I ought to fill you in with what's happening right now at Camp Green Lake. I'm afraid that some weird things have happened ...

TASK

Now that you have imagined that you are Stanley, you should have a better insight into his character. Share your letter with a partner and then read theirs. Try and suggest changes and improvements by asking yourself these questions:

- Does the language sound as though it was written by Stanley?
- Are there any important details missing?
- Is anything included that Stanley might have decided not to tell his mother?

Two worlds merge?

Chapters 40–42

As we near the end of the novel, much more information has been revealed to the reader. We are able to make all kinds of connections between the two narratives in the novel. We begin to realise that the two worlds will merge. Certainly, it would be a very neat way to conclude Stanley's story and might even break the 'curse' of Elya Yelnats.

Could the thumb-shaped mountain 'Big Thumb' be connected to God's Thumb on which Stanley's great grandfather sought refuge after he had been robbed by Kissin' Kate Barlow?

You are now going to gather some evidence as you piece together the mysterious link behind the two storylines.

TASK

Draw a copy of the following table. Using the example above to start you off, add more examples of clues and coincidences which seem to suggest that the narratives are about to converge.

Evidence	Link between stories

TASK

Imagine that you are Louis Sachar. Write a letter to your publishers, explaining your need to use juxtaposed storylines. Try and persuade them that this particular narrative choice is central to your novel. Below is a suggestion for how you could start your letter.

Dear Editor,

Thank you for showing interest in my ideas for the narrative structure of my novel <u>Holes</u>.

I felt that I needed to juxtapose the story of Stanley digging his first hole with that of Elya Yelnats' experiences with Myra and Madame Zeroni. This is because there are definite links between these different stories. You see, Elya Yelnats is Stanley's . . .

Stanley at Camp Green

Kissing Kate Barlow

Yellow-spotted lizards!

Chapters 43–47

Chapters 43–47

TASK

Re-read the following extract from Chapter 45.

Text mark your extract, paying particular attention to:

- Sachar's use of tension devices
- Stanley's thoughts and feelings
- Your reaction as a reader when you read the extract

Zero sat as still as a statue.

A second lizard crawled up over the side of the suitcase and stopped less than an inch away from Zero's little finger.

Stanley was afraid to look, and afraid not to. He wondered if he should try to scramble out of the hole before the lizards turned on him, but he didn't want to cause any commotion.

The second lizard crawled across Zero's fingers and halfway up his arm.

It occurred to Stanley that the lizards were probably on the suitcase when he handed it to Zero.

"There's another one!" gasped Mr. Pendanski. He shined the flashlight on the box of Frosted Flakes, which lay on its side beside Stanley's hole. A lizard was crawling out of it.

The light also illuminated Stanley's hole. He glanced downward and had to force himself to suppress a scream. He was standing in a lizard nest. He felt the scream explode inside him.

He could see six lizards. There were three on the ground, two on his left leg, and one on his right sneaker.

He tried to remain very still. Something was crawling up the back of his neck.

Three other counsellors approached the area. Stanley heard one say, "What's going –" and then whisper, "Oh my God."

"What do we do?" asked Mr. Pendanski.

"We wait," said the Warden. "It won't be very long."

"At least we'll have a body to give to that woman," said Mr. Pendanski…

…Stanley felt tiny claws dig into the side of his face as the lizard pulled itself off his neck and up past his chin.

"It won't be long now," the Warden said.

Stanley could hear his heart beat. Each beat told him he was still alive, at least for one more second.

Destiny or coincidence?

Chapters
48–50

'When the shoes fell from the sky, he remembered thinking that destiny had struck him. Now, he thought so again. It was more than a coincidence. It had to be destiny.'

So thinks Stanley in Chapter 42.

TASK

With a partner, discuss your feelings about fate or destiny. Have you ever felt that something was 'just meant to be'? Have you ever felt that something was completely unavoidable and that, whatever you did, your fate had already been decided for you?

That is how Stanley feels about his life since he was arrested for the 'theft' of the sneakers. However, he accepts his destiny.

'He was glad Zero put the shoes on the parked car. He was glad they fell from the overpass and hit him on the head.'

In spite of Stanley's poverty, weight and unlucky streak, this is the mark of a true hero, to accept his destiny.

TASK

Look back through the novel and search for references to fate or destiny.

The Woodpecker Song

Louis Sachar ends his novel with an interesting choice – he provides the reader with the final verse of 'The Woodpecker Song', which appears at different points in the novel. This is a deliberate narrative technique by the writer. Below are the three verses and their chapter references:

Chapters 3 and 39

"If only, if only," the woodpecker sighs,
"The bark on the tree was just a little bit softer."
While the wolf waits below, hungry and lonely,
He cries to the moo-oo-oon,
"If only, if only."

Chapter 7

"If only, if only," the woodpecker sighs,
"The bark on the tree was as soft as the skies."
While the wolf waits below, hungry and lonely,
Crying to the moo-oo-oon,
"If only, if only."

Chapter 50

"If only, if only," the moon speaks no reply;
Reflecting the sun and all that's gone by.
Be strong my weary wolf, turn around boldly.
Fly high, my baby bird,
My angel, my only.

TASK

Read the different verses of 'The Woodpecker Song' on page 72 and answer the following questions:

❶ How do the verses relate to the chapters in which they appear?

❷ How is a sense of longing created by this song? Who longs for what?

❸ What do you notice about the use of images in the song?

❹ What do you notice about the use of rhythm and how it helps to create a tone of longing? Remember that Elya told Sarah that it rhymed in Latvian.

❺ How has the verse been changed on each occasion, and what is the effect of this change?

Poets often use metaphors to invite the reader to draw comparisons between things, or to add depth and colour to their presentation of people and things. Could the wolf and the woodpecker in the verse be linked to the characters in *Holes*?

TASK

Work with your partner to annotate the last verse of 'The Woodpecker Song'. Consider the following as you contribute to the annotation:

● That Hector's mother is half-singing, half-humming the song.

● Why the moon 'speaks no reply.'

● The meaning of the second line of the verse to the singer.

● How a new positive note is introduced into the verse.

● Who the 'baby bird' could be here.

● How this last version of 'The Woodpecker Song' is a resolution of the two narratives of *Holes*. What does it suggest about Stanley and Hector's futures?

● Does the last line suggest that the curse is broken?

Prepare your ideas and annotations on the third stanza of 'The Woodpecker Song' and present them as a formal oral report to the rest of the class. Remember to make your points clearly, providing clear evidence in the form of quotations from the verse. Explain how the quotations relate to your ideas.

'Holes' – a novel full of connections and coincidences!
Can you add any more?

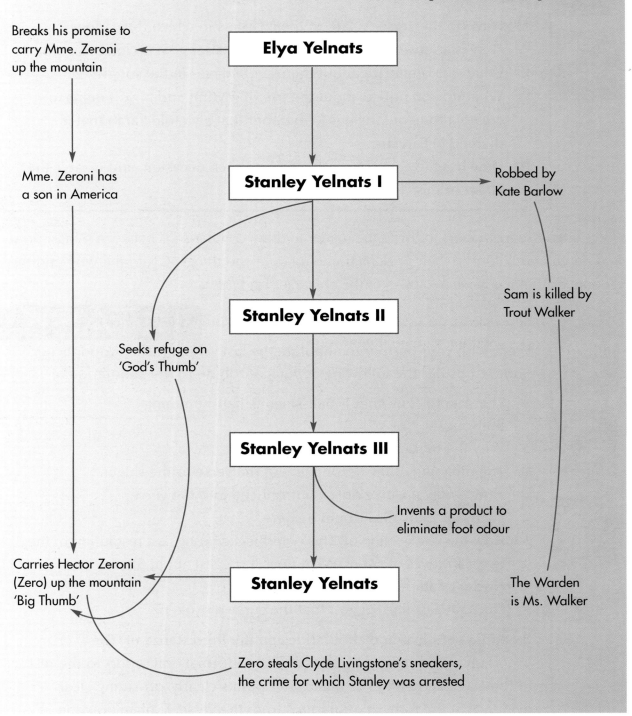

Breaks his promise to carry Mme. Zeroni up the mountain

Elya Yelnats

Mme. Zeroni has a son in America

Stanley Yelnats I

Robbed by Kate Barlow

Sam is killed by Trout Walker

Seeks refuge on 'God's Thumb'

Stanley Yelnats II

Stanley Yelnats III

Invents a product to eliminate foot odour

Carries Hector Zeroni (Zero) up the mountain 'Big Thumb'

Stanley Yelnats

The Warden is Ms. Walker

Zero steals Clyde Livingstone's sneakers, the crime for which Stanley was arrested

TASK

At the beginning of the unit you made some predictions of what would happen in the novel. Review your early predictions now using the table below:

My prediction	What actually happened
1 I thought that Stanley...	1 In the end, Stanley...

TASK

You also asked some questions after the early chapters.

❶ Review the questions now and consider how they have been answered.

❷ Discuss the answers to your questions with a partner. Does anything remain unanswered?

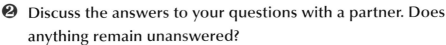

❸ Share your ideas with the rest of the class. How effectively does Louis Sachar prepare you for the way the novel ends?

In this unit you have had the opportunity to practise a whole variety of reading strategies, such as:

- Reading backwards and forwards
- Questioning
- Empathising
- Visualising
- Inferring and deducing

- Annotating or text marking
- Tracing narrative structure
- Investigating narrative technique
- Making notes

You will be able to use what you have learned in both your private reading and in your approach to the texts which you read and write about in class.

UNIT 4 Lost voices

In this unit you will learn about the following key objectives:

Complex sentences – how to construct more complex sentences and when it might be appropriate to use them in your writing

Anticipate reader reaction – working out how you want your reader to react to your writing

Narrative commentary – reflecting on your writing as you draft and complete a dramatic monologue

Collaborative presentation – developing a dramatic presentation by working closely with others

Your writing will be based on real events that happened to real children just like you. As you develop your dramatic monologues, you will be taking on a role, first as an adult, then as a child, and writing as if you are these characters.

As you write, you will be asked to work in pairs, groups and as a class to create a Writer's Forum in which you will share ideas, read each other's work and suggest improvements to your monologues. Any notes, first ideas and plans will be kept by you in a jotter.

You will be striving to create the maximum impact on your audience by preparing a dramatic presentation of your monologues so that the 'lost voices' of these characters can be finally heard.

Problems and solutions

TASK

❶ You are going to study a range of facts and opinions about conditions in England and Australia in the 1950s.

❷ Working with a partner, read the 'Statement card' handout based on conditions in English or Australian society in the 1950s. Discuss the following questions together in a pair:

❏ Is the information on your card a fact or an opinion?

❏ Does your card tell you about: the children of the 1940s/50s; Australia at the time; or the charities set up to deal with orphans?

❸ Read out your card to the rest of the class and listen as other pairs do the same.

❹ When you have heard all of the statements, work again in pairs and discuss what you have found out and what you think are the main problems.

❺ In your jotter, briefly write down three crucial problems that the children face.

TASK

Study the pictures and fact boxes on pages 78 and 79.

Historical facts

1939–1945	Second World War
1945	Labour Government in power, Clement Attlee Prime Minister
1952	Death of King George
1952	First nuclear bomb tests carried out
1953	Elizabeth II crowned Queen of England

Orphanages and institutions

Before 1950, examples of residential care for children were: the industrial school, borstal, orphanage and reformatory. These institutions had much the same approach to children and their care. There were few comforts, the systems were strict, routines were enforced, manual work was harsh and hard, and punishments were sometimes severe.

Attitudes and beliefs

- Concern over the overcrowded, slum conditions in many cities

- Belief in the importance of the British Empire (British owned and controlled lands overseas)

- Pride in being British, but concern over post-war conditions in Britain

- Charitable organisations, often run by church groups, existed to organise the care of the poor and the orphaned

- Courage and endurance were considered to be very important qualities

- Idle and abandoned children were considered to be almost dangerous, posing a threat to society. The institutions were meant to 'save' these children and make them 'respectable'.

Child migration

There have been many British child migration schemes over the centuries. The last phase, and the most famous, was between 1947 to 1967. Opinions differ on the numbers involved, but it appears to have involved about 3,000 children.

Unaccompanied young girls and boys who were already in care were sent overseas and placed in Australian orphanages before joining the ordinary workforce. The average age was 9.4 years. Some adults alive today have good memories of what happened to them, but many recall the hardships and the sense of being abandoned and far from home.

In 1954, 38 orphaned and abandoned children left England on board the SS Esperance Bay, travelling from Southampton to Sydney, Australia.

TASK

❶ Working in groups of four, imagine that you are members of an important committee of adults who make decisions about children in orphanages. You might want to give your committee a name like: The Charitable Board of Guardians.

❷ Stay in role and discuss the following. From what you have discovered so far, what do you think can best be done for these children? Remember to begin your discussions in the first person with 'I think…' to show that you are speaking as an adult member of this charitable group.

❸ Share your findings with the rest of the class. You may want to do this by 'spotlighting' – re-enacting a small but essential piece of your drama work or by reporting back out of role.

Now you have come up with some dramatised solutions to the problems at that time, compare it to what actually happened: for over a century, up to the end of the 1950s, several charitable organisations had been sending children from poverty-stricken and deprived homes to children's homes abroad. Many were sent to Australian orphanages and farm schools. A government report drawn up in 1951 revealed that a total of 2100 orphaned or abandoned children were part of various emigration schemes to Australia between 1947 and 1951.

Finding an adult's voice

First person

Working with your handout, look at the example which converts a sentence from third to first person. Remind yourselves of the difference between the first, second and third person. Then, complete the sheet to make sure that you have understood the importance of being able to write in a consistent way throughout your dramatic monologues.

Now that you know what happened to the orphaned children you are ready to begin your first dramatic monologue. You are going to pretend to be one of the adults involved with the charities as they go through a process of decision making, selection and organisation of their writing.

Brainstorm: Who would the hat fit?

❶ Study the illustrations below which show a wide range of hats. They represent possible adult roles, such as 'a lord' or 'a magistrate'. They will help you to prepare for your brainstorm.

❷ As a whole class, brainstorm ideas to create a list of all the types of adults who might have been involved with the charities and orphanages.

❸ Collect these ideas on a piece of sugar paper that can be displayed in the future.

You now need to choose your own character whose monologue you are going to write. To do this, you will need to make some decisions about your character's background. Use the box on page 81 to help you.

- Name
- Position in society – how wealthy, powerful, influential is your character?
- Family – what sort of family background do they have?
- Experience – where have they lived or worked? What connections do they have with needy children?
- Attitudes – what do they think about the poor and deprived people in society?
- Voice – how do they speak? What sort of words and phrases do they use?

TASK

The information below will help you to consider the voices and attitudes of the adults concerned.

Some of the people who helped to run charitable organisations were people with the time and desire to work voluntarily for the poor. These included church leaders, members of Boards of Guardians of Orphanages and other adults responsible for the children's welfare.

One child migrant remembers being called in to see the Mother Superior (the head of the children's home) expecting to be told off. Her words were, 'Have a seat, my child,' and she then talked about him being sent to Australia. She said that he had been chosen and that it was a special opportunity and not a punishment. But that night in bed, he cried about it.

Many of the people in positions of power believed it was a great and noble project because poor children, with no hope or future, were going to a land rich in opportunity and resources; a land which needed children from the British Empire.

TASK

❶ To help you, complete the 'Role on the wall' handout and begin to explore your character's voice by completing the speech bubbles around your drawing.

❷ Share your ideas on your characters with the rest of your class, explaining your decisions carefully.

❸ Make a class display of the characters you have created.

Put on the spot

TASK

❶ In pairs, quickly remind yourselves about what a dramatic monologue is. If necessary check at the start of the unit.

❷ Read the invitation below. Your character has been called to the Board of Guardians of the Midchester Orphanage. The orphanage has been considering the problems of overcrowding and deprivation of children in the Midchester area. You are seen as an expert whose advice will be carefully considered. Your speech to the board will take the form of a dramatic monologue.

*Midchester Board of Guardians
requests the attendance of*

_____

*at their annual meeting
on
8th November, 1948
at 7.00pm*

TASK

❶ Remember that for your speech you are writing as an educated adult who will be using more complex sentences and vocabulary. Read the example below which converts simple sentences into a single, complex sentence.

❷ Working in pairs, discuss the differences between these two sentences; what has been changed, what has been added?

Simple sentences: I travel around the country. I see poor children. They are in need.
Linking into a complex sentence: As I travel around the country, I see too many poverty-stricken children, who are in dire need.

The complex sentence has linked three simple sentences by beginning with the preposition 'As' which creates a noun clause, and this explains when and where the children are seen. The final clause 'who are in dire need' adds more detail about the children. The adjectives 'poverty-stricken' and 'dire' strengthen our understanding of the level of need.

TASK

You are now going to move into groups to begin the opening paragraph of your monologue to the Board of Guardians. You could use one of your speech bubbles from the handout and expand those words into a paragraph. But remember, you must attract the attention of your listeners from the very beginning.

❶ Read the possibilities below.

❷ Then begin writing your paragraph. It needs to contain at least three complex sentences.

'Well, ladies and gentlemen, where should I begin?'

'Once in a lifetime, such an opportunity can arise!'

'Imagine, if you can, a world where these children…'

'Do you want to change a child's life today?'

TASK

❶ Working in pairs, read aloud your opening sentences to your partner. Listen for the way in which he or she has grabbed the attention of the audience in the opening lines. What do you notice? Can you suggest improvements? Repeat the process with your partner's work.

❷ In the Writer's Forum, read out your opening sentences and explain to the class why you chose those particular words, phrases, clauses and sentences.

The unfinished sentences bag

'I ask you to consider the following:
………..…, …….....……, …………..';
'When I look back at my own experience,
I realise…'
'However, we must be wary of…'
'………and, as a result
of this,…'

Explain yourself!

If you are going to convince someone that you have a terrific idea which they really ought to implement, you have to be able to explain yourself clearly and persuade people that you are right. To do this, there are a number of techniques you can use.

TASK

❶ Work in groups of three. **A** and **B** will be involved in a paired improvisation and **C** will be the observer.

❷ Let **A** be a teenager of about 13, and **B** the teenager's parent. **A** wants to stay out later than 8.00pm at a friend's house but the parent wants him/her home by that time. Improvise the situation while **C** observes and notes down exactly how each tries to persuade the other.

❸ All of the **C**s in the class report back to the whole class on the persuasive techniques they have observed.

In your feedback, you may uncover more verbal techniques which you could add to the list showing ways of persuading others.

Possible persuasive techniques

- Non-verbal gestures, eye contact, facial expressions, body language:
- Verbal
- Rhetorical questions, for example, 'Why shouldn't I?', 'What's your problem?' or 'Do you expect me to believe that?'
- Justification – 'Well, I don't think there's anything wrong with being out after 8.00pm.'
- Plea for sympathy – 'It will only be for just this one time.'
- Appeal to a sense of justice – 'Other people don't get treated like this.'
- Threat – 'You can't make me!'
- Reasoned argument – 'It seems to me that at 13, I should be trusted a little more.'

All of these techniques are ways of developing an argument. This is exactly what you require for your dramatic monologue to the Board of Guardians.

Talking into writing

The essence of the dramatic monologue is the way in which the talker (in this case, your adult expert) gradually reveals more and more about themselves, often by addressing the reader or listener directly. To do this well, you need to plan very carefully.

TASK

❶ Take a technique from your paired improvisations; for example, an appeal to a sense of justice. In your dramatic monologue, it might look like this:

'Ladies and gentlemen, these children deserve your intervention to provide them with a better life.'

This is a powerful opening sentence to a paragraph but in order to fully develop your argument in your dramatic monologue, you need to develop it by addressing the reader more directly. This can be done by exploring the internal thoughts the speaker has about the monologue. So, the opening sentence might become:

'Ladies and gentlemen (yes, that's a polite, formal way to begin), these children deserve your intervention (no, perhaps a word like 'pity' might be more powerful) to provide them with a better life (I like the ending because it suggests optimism).'

❷ Develop your monologues with this added 'internal voice' openly reflecting on the power of the language choices. Use the following points to continue:
- ❏ Members of the Board of Guardians have the power and authority to send children away
- ❏ Without them, the children will continue to suffer in their present conditions
- ❏ It is urgent

❸ The paragraph might look like this when it is re-worked. You need to put the internal voice in the spaces in brackets:

'Ladies and gentlemen (yes, that's a polite, formal way to begin), these children deserve your intervention (no, perhaps a word like 'pity' might be more powerful) to provide them with a better life (I like the ending because it suggests optimism). Only you, (.......) as Members of the Board of Guardians, have the power and authority (......) to send children to a bright future (......). Without your support, these children will continue to suffer (.......) in their present conditions. It is a matter of the utmost urgency (........).'

Now you have a complete paragraph with supporting detail – very persuasive! However, this paragraph is unconnected to the next paragraph. Connectives are like strong chains which link paragraphs together giving your writing strength and shape. Here are some connecting phrases which you could use as you plan: 'Another point to consider..., Furthermore…, You may like to consider...'

❹ Work in pairs to prepare your next four paragraphs using ideas from the improvisation. Don't forget the connectives!

❺ Share one example of the way you have taken a topic sentence, developed it and thought about a suitable connective.

Buddy critics

One of the most effective ways of improving your writing is to work with a trusted partner or buddy, who can listen to or read your work on dramatic monologues, and give you valuable and constructive feedback.

The focus at this point is on ways of concluding your dramatic monologues. An effective conclusion simply:

- re-states the basic general argument
- uses a few, brief sentences
- avoids introducing anything new

TASK

Practise being a 'buddy critic' by working in pairs to either read out loud or listen and respond to a selection of concluding sentences. If you are working as the buddy critic, you will need to pass judgement on what you hear. For instance, you might say:

> That was very powerful at the beginning but I thought it was a little too long

> Remember, these children are from very poor backgrounds. Did you know that some of them can hardly write their own names! Perhaps they could receive an education abroad at the farm school? Who knows what the possibilities might be?

'That sounds a bit short and I didn't really understand what you meant. Can you make it a bit clearer?'

or:

'That was very powerful at the beginning but I thought it was a little too long.'

English Works

Take it in turns to be the buddy or the reader for the following concluding sentences:

- So, Ladies and Gentlemen, that's about it really.
- In conclusion, might I take this opportunity to re-emphasise the points I made earlier.
- Ladies and Gentlemen, these children are poor, powerless and anxious for a new life. Only you can help them. Only you can transform their lives!
- Remember, these children are from very poor backgrounds. Did you know that some of them can hardly write their own names! Perhaps they could receive an education abroad at the farm school? Who knows what the possibilities might be?

TASK

Use the ideas you have been practising to write your own conclusion to your dramatic monologue. Begin by jotting down the four or five essential points you have made in you monologue so far.

Now that you have your fully drafted dramatic monologue, it is time to work together again as buddy critics to really polish it so that it has as much impact as possible on your audience.

TASK

You and your buddy critic are going to help each other by using some of the following techniques:

- Swapping your dramatic monologue with your buddy critic
- Underlining any words, sentences, connectives, paragraphs or development points which you feel are not quite effective enough
- Briefly explaining your point in the margin next to your underlining
- Reading aloud a short passage or sentence so that you can both consider its effect

The moment of truth

The time has come to put your dramatic monologue to the test. You will find out just how effective your carefully crafted language really is when you use it before a live audience. Your dramatic monologue will be the introduction to a piece of improvised drama on the subject of the orphaned children and their fate.

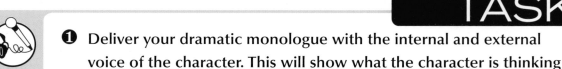

❶ Deliver your dramatic monologue with the internal and external voice of the character. This will show what the character is thinking and how he or she is trying to use the language to manipulate the audience.

❷ Deliver the dramatic monologue without the internal voice so that you can move into the improvisation.

To improve it, try to deliver your monologue without looking at your sheets. You will probably find this hard at first, but persevere. It is much more effective if you say it instead of reading it. This means learning it! Use the build-up exercise below to help you.

In order to increase the tension and to prepare you, there are a number of build-up exercises:

❏ Decide if you are brave enough to be the first person in your class to try a small section of your dramatic monologue. One of you will need to volunteer to work in role with your teacher to demonstrate what is required to the rest of the group.

❏ As the first monologue is read through, observe the listener carefully. His or her response is most important. To listen actively, you will need to maintain eye contact and use gestures and facial expressions to demonstrate that you understand.

❏ As the dramatic monologue ends, the listener will need a key question to move into the improvised section of the work. Think what your key question might be and write it down in your jotter.

TASK

1 Now it is your turn to prepare for the final presentation. Working in groups of four, have one pair read and actively listen. The other pair needs to observe and note down the successful points it sees.

2 Swap over so that the observers have a chance to present and be observed.

3 Re-convene as a whole group and suggest the most effective ways of presenting and actively listening.

TASK

1 Move into a forum theatre where the whole group can observe and comment on the dramatic action. When you are ready, move into the centre with your external voice dramatic monologue. Put your case to the Board of Governors who will ask you some searching questions afterwards.

2 Move back into your original pairs. Quickly decide on the memorable moments from the dramatisation of the monologues. What were the key moments and what were the strengths of the monologues?

3 Jot down one positive comment and place it on the display.

4 There is one voice which has not yet been heard. Can you identify it from this short extract?

'I had no idea what they were sending me to.'

Finding the child

You have looked at the problems caused by the growing numbers of orphans from the adult's point of view. You are now going to 'step into the shoes' of the children involved. What was it like from their point of view? How do you think they felt about being transported 13,000 miles away from England? In your second dramatic monologue, you will be giving an imaginary child a voice to tell his or her tale.

TASK

❶ In pairs, remind each other of the difference between simple and complex sentences. Decide on an explanation of a complex sentence and give an example!

❷ Write a sentence together that sounds as if a child is speaking his or her thoughts aloud. Share these with your class, and listen carefully to the many voices created.

❸ Discuss with your partner whether each sentence successfully reproduced a child's voice. Which were the most effective, and why?

❹ Now study the boxes below and make a copy of them. Your task is to change each sentence to make it sound more convincing as part of a child's monologue. Remember, you are trying to create the voice of one of the children from the orphanage. The 'Help box' suggests some of the aspects of language you will need to consider.

'Although conditions were appalling at home, there is nothing worse than lying in this dormitory wondering what the adults here are planning for us.'

'Whenever I recall my Mother, I perceive that conditions were harsh for her, and for my brothers.'

'The Home is bearable for the majority of the year, but I would prefer better food, better accommodation, and more regular visits from my family.'

Help box

Think about:

Vocabulary – which words would a child use?

Abbreviations – which words might be shortened to echo the child's accent?

Sentences – how will you punctuate sentences to sound like a child speaking?

The extracts below are adapted from the accounts of real people who experienced life in the orphanages or children's homes in England, the journey to Australia, and life as a child migrant there.

I was put in the children's home after Florrie died. She was my foster mother, see, an' she was old, older than my real Mother I think. I remember seein' this other woman sometimes – fur coat an' beautiful – she came to visit me, an' I'm sure she was my real Mother. But after the war, I was moved, and then they chose me to go to Australia.

My Mother didn't want to give me up, you know, she just didn't have much choice. There was this man, a different one, and he wouldn't have me an' my brother when they got together, an' he always promised her he'd get us out once they were settled, but it never happened. I keep writing, and I will even when I get to Australia.

This woman asked me if I wanted to go to Australia, an' I says 'yes', 'cos it sounded good, an' somethin' different... but it was the worst thing ev' 'appened to me. Us kids couldn't hardly imagine it, and it was wrong to ask us. We knew nothin'. Sendin' us out there – from the moment I arrived I wish't I was back where I knew places an' people and things...

It was a shock to be there. In England we were in a town, surrounded by people. We saw people on our way to school, we could go out an' buy Granny Smiths apples and things, five for a penny, and I remember the Italian prisoners of war sweepin' the streets... but out there was wild, open spaces, it was out in the bush they call it, all scrub land, and the school, the church and the convent all together in the middle with nothin' around for miles...

I was told the reason for exporting me, like, was 'cos me Mother was always sayin' she'd visit, but she never did, so they reckoned I'd be better off in Australia.

In pairs, take it in turns to read the extracts aloud to each other. Then choose three that you feel really show what the children experienced. Read these aloud as a class.

You are now ready to plan and begin to write your second monologue: memories and events from the child's point of view. You will be in groups, working on your own piece, but also sharing ideas at times with a partner.

❶ Using your 'The child speaks' handout, develop your character. Complete the speech bubbles and sketch out a face for your child. This is the beginning of the monologue, so start with the child's experiences in England. Remember what you learnt from the activities about recreating a child's voice, and use the extracts on page 91 to help you include feelings and experiences.

❷ Share your results with a partner, and listen to their ideas. Should any words or sentences be changed to make the child's voice more convincing?

❸ Now use your 'Sentence to paragraph' handout to help you write your first paragraphs, by expanding the sentences from your speech bubbles.

❶ Your group now needs to plan a 'reading of parts' from each of your pieces of writing. Choose a sentence each that you feel you could read aloud and decide as a group the order in which they are to be read.

❷ Present this to the class and listen carefully. When the reading is complete, discuss in your group which extracts made you feel particular sympathy for the child involved.

Building stories

Now you have chosen your character and begun to create the 'voice' of this particular child, you are ready to plan and write the whole of the story that makes up your dramatic monologue. To make your writing particularly effective, remember to consider three elements: reader response, structure, and descriptive detail.

Reader response

Every piece of writing has an intended audience: a reader, or an audience who listens to the reading.

TASK

With a partner, study the extract below. It is part of a diary written by Zlata, a girl who lived through the terrible events in Sarajevo, in the former Yugoslavia. One of you needs to read it aloud to the other. Discuss what it makes you feel and think both as the reader and 'audience'.

❚❚ Two shells exploded in the street and one in the market. Mummy was nearby at the time. She ran to Grandma's and Grandad's. Daddy and I were beside ourselves because she hadn't come home. I saw some of it on TV but I still can't believe what I actually saw. It's unbelievable. I've got a lump in my throat and a knot in my tummy. HORRIBLE. They're taking the wounded to the hospital. It's a MADHOUSE. We kept going to the window hoping to see Mummy, but she wasn't back. They released a list of the dead and wounded. Daddy and I were tearing our hair out. We didn't know what had happened to her. Was she alive? ❚❚

TASK

❶ Read the comments on your handout and add your own responses around the text as a narrative commentary describing the effects on the reader.

❷ As you prepare to write the next part of your monologue, think about *your* audience and how you want them to respond. Parts of your writing will be read aloud in a dramatic presentation to the class – how will you get them to understand and feel sympathy for your character? Make a list of some ideas in your jotter.

Structure

You will have noticed that the extracts on page 91 describing the children's experiences are in four phases: Life in England; the journey; arrival in Australia; living in Australia. These could provide the structure for your story, to give it a beginning, a middle and an end.

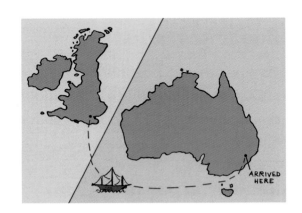

Descriptive detail

TASK

Using your 'Story maps' handout, plan the next stages of your character's journey in more detail, as they begin their journey by sea and begin life in a new land far away.

❶ Inside the outline of the ship on your handout, write words or phrases that describe the specific memories your character might have had as they left England and experienced the journey. Use the checklist at the sides to help you gather lots of ideas.

❷ Inside the outline map of Australia, collect words and phrases that describe experiences when your character arrived and was sent to an orphanage or 'farm school'.

❸ Share your first ideas with a partner, and add further detail after this conversation.

❹ Using these lists as a guide, write your paragraphs to continue your child's monologue.

TASK

❶ When you have written several paragraphs, work with a partner to 'test out' reader response, structure and descriptive detail. Read your work to each other, one at a time.

❷ When you have listened to your partner's work, jot down what you noticed about feelings created, the structure and the detail. Share your responses.

Endings

As you reach the end of your monologue, you need to consider how to create an effective ending, so that your reader or audience is left with a sense of completion; a feeling that the child has said all that needs to be said at that point in their lives. Writing 'THE END' is not enough!

TASK

In small groups, study these three extracts, and decide:

- **What feelings are aroused in the reader?**
- **Does the final sentence provide a satisfactory ending in your opinion?**

▌▌ The day came at last when I was allowed to leave. The sun shone as always, my clothes seemed to stick to my body, and no-one waved as the bus pulled away. ▌▌

▌▌ My real friend was called Peter, and he'd come from the north somewhere. He told us the best stories. ▌▌

▌▌ I often wondered about my Mother. One day perhaps... ▌▌

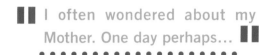

TASK

In your group, brainstorm several ways of creating final paragraphs that will help you to build up to an effective ending. Use the ideas here to help you.

A definite ending for a definite time
'The last day was the worst really... I knew it was over then; there was nothing more I could do, and nothing more to say.'

Final reflection
'When I look back at that time, I remember...'

Letting the reader wonder
'And so my new life began, still far from home, but better in many ways. I was no longer the lonely child who had landed all those months ago at the harbour side. I was beginning again...'

Complete your first draft of your monologue, by working independently on your own ending. You could try out various styles, share them with a partner, and then decide which one works best for the voice and character of your child.

Look back at your 'Zlata's diary' handout. The comments identified the reader's response to the words chosen. Decide:

● What emotions you want to share
● What response you are aiming for
● What words and phrases you could choose to create these

Sadness   **Pride and independence**

Hopelessness

Acceptance

Sympathy   **Hope and optimism**

When you have all completed your drafts by choosing and writing your endings, share two of them in a whole class activity. Two volunteers will be needed to write up the final part of their monologue for the whole class to see. This could be put on to acetate, a whiteboard or sugar paper.

❶ Study each piece. Read it quietly to yourself.
❷ Discuss the extract with a partner, identifying the emotions expressed and aroused. What do you learn of the child's life, feelings and character?
❸ Share some of these ideas as a whole class by writing responses around the extract. Volunteers will be needed to come to the front and write a comment each.

Giving voice

You are approaching the point where your child's 'voice' will need to go public; to be heard and recognised. Before that happens, you need to be sure that the character you have created through its voice is authentic and credible. To achieve this, look very closely at how the 'voice' works: the words, phrases and even the punctuation you have used can bring your character to life vocally.

TASK

Read the extracts below. The first is a draft version of a 'voice' and the second suggests ways in which the 'voice' might be developed.

This is the voice of 'Tim', a 12 year-old cockney lad who was sent from one of the London orphanages to a farm in Young, NSW, about 200 miles from Sydney.

Here is the first attempt at Tim's voice:

> I arrived over here on a huge boat. We were not expecting what we found. The heat was unbearable on the docks that day and I thought Sydney harbour was wonderful. But I didn't know that we would be going into the outback. It was miles and miles and miles and as we travelled it became drier and hotter and more fly blown.

However, Tim speaks in a dialect of English and, consequently, he adapts the usual rules governing Standard English. This is a re-drafted version of Tim's voice:

A Tim is likely to speak in a colloquial dialect so words like 'arrived' need to be simplified into 'cum'

B His accent usually omits the 'h' when it is followed by a vowel; so, words like 'home' and 'heat' would become 'ome' and 'eat'

C Verbally, the past tense verbs such as 'was' and 'were' can sometimes be used without reference to the person. For example, 'We were…' can become 'We was…' and 'It was…' can become 'It were…'

> I <u>cum</u> over 'ere on a boat as big as me street back <u>'ome</u>. We <u>was</u> not expectin' it to be like it was. The 'eat was the first thing but Sydney harbour were a picture. None of us knew we was going bush, though. It was miles and miles an' the further we went; the 'otter it got. The flies was everywhere.

TASK

❶ Work in a pair and read both extract versions from page 97 aloud to each other. Try to get some sense of the rhythm of Tim's voice and, as you do, try to add some gestures and facial expressions so that Tim begins to really come to life in your versions.

❷ Now, read through the following longer first draft of Tim's monologue and then use your jotters to revise it and to text mark your changes as in the example on page 97.

❚❚ When we finally arrived at the work farm, we were all very surprised to find that there was a river and cabins and even other children there, too. Initially, we felt a little unsure about what we were supposed to do but, as we settled in, there were plenty of things to keep us busy. We still missed England terribly but, we were often so tired from all the work, that we didn't really think of home until the evening. Then, as the sun went down and the cicadas began clicking, we used to lay awake, thinking. ❚❚

TASK

❶ Now, it is time to return to your own dramatic monologues. Swap your work with a partner, read each other's and suggest three examples where your partner might review and improve their writing.

❷ In preparation for your final presentations make sure that your dramatic monologues are finished.

❸ Choose two examples from your partner's work that you have reviewed and improved. Explain what you have done to the rest of the group.

The tension mounts

You will soon be presenting your dramatic monologues to an audience. This might be an audience of your class members, another class, parents or even, perhaps, younger children. There are many ways you can add dramatic impact to your monologues but one of the first things to consider is whether you want to work as a pair or as part of a larger group.

If you are lucky, you may have access to a drama room for your presentations and, if this is the case, you will be able to make more use of the space, lighting and perhaps even costume.

TASK

Consider the ways of presenting your monologue by reading the various possibilities on this page.

The illustration above simply recreates the two characters, places them side by side and presents the monologues consecutively. You should consider the following in your preparations:

- Do the two characters ever look at one another?
- If so, how is this done? E.g. slowly, with expressions?
- Would you surround the characters with any props or pictures? What effect would you be trying to create?
- Will you read the monologues or learn them and deliver them live?

You could attempt to recreate the voices by organising people to read the dramatic monologues on to tape. The presentation could be in the form of a radio documentary which you prepare by scripting and interject with extracts from the tape. You would need to make decisions concerning:

- Who would create a powerful 'voice' for the two characters?
- What else would you write into a script to make it seem like a documentary for the audience?

If you decide to work with a group, your options for presentation are increased. You might, for instance, decide to use some of the group to recreate tableaux as a dramatic backdrop to the monologues. You would need to decide:

- What images would serve as a balance to the messages in the monologues
- At what points in the delivery you would change the tableaux. Why would you do this?

If you want to be really daring, you could take the monologues and cut them up into a number of different sections. Then, rather like a modernist painting, you could share out the different cut up voices and read them aloud to your audience. You would need to consider:

- The order in which you read the sections of monologue
- How you would move about the presentation area
- Whether you would use props, costumes or even music to create an effect

Or, perhaps you could go completely into character and attempt to bring the voices to life through careful consideration of costume, movement, voice, props and lighting so that the audience are treated to the 'real thing'. You will need to learn your dramatic monologue off by heart for this version of the presentation.

The lost voices

❶ You need to get the mood just right for this lesson. Sit quietly, on your own, for a few moments and think about three things you want to achieve by the end. For instance, you might want to portray a particular emotion in your voice or body language.

❷ As you do this, look at the examples below and on page 102 of dramatic monologues by various fictitious characters and the illustrations from their lives. Although these characters are imaginary, the events really did happen. How can you and your class best bring their stories to life?

Lady Fairbridge (Standing addressing a group who face her)

'This is a project which can bring only good. New life, new hope and new beginnings for children who, as I speak, have none of these things.'

Sarah (13) (Sitting on a stump in the outback)

'What I actually miss are the times when we used to play down our street. There was a great crowd of us and we'd have skipping ropes from washing lines and all the girls would try to get in on the skipping at the same time. Our record was nineteen.'

Sir Toby Muncaster (At a gentleman's club – oak panelled walls and comfy leather chair – he has cigar in hand)

'Blue skies, clean air, the great outdoors; what a wonderful way to live. I wish I had had the opportunities we are offering to these young people.'

Brian (15) (Sitting facing an interviewer who is taking notes)

'The work was hard and hot but, in the end, I got used to it. We would get up at dawn and work on the farm until about six at night. Winters was cold at night but lovely during the day. Summer was just hot all the time. I never got paid nothing for all them hours.'

Jack (10) (On his bed in the dormitory)

'I wonder where me brother went to. He was two years younger than me and he got scared on his own. I asked to stay together but we got separated. I'd love to be able to see him again. Whenever I asked, they just told me they didn't know where he was.'

Betty (35) (Standing at the empty dockside looking out to sea)

'They took my Gloria when she was born. They said that she would have a better life than she could ever have with me. Girls like me weren't supposed to make good mothers but I loved her. I loved her better than anyone else could have.'

Mary (18) (Imagining her mother at the dockside as she tries to sleep at night)

'I sometimes wonder what me mother must have been like. I have to imagine her because I ain't got no pictures or nothing. I think she must have been a lady because I got this lovely hair.'

Appreciation

As you watch the dramatic monologues being presented, you will need to be more than a passive member of the audience. Of course, people will want you to listen carefully and support the presenters who are, after all, taking a risk by performing their work before you. However, in order to be an active listener, you need to think critically about what you are observing.

TASK

❶ In your jotters, quickly copy out the boxes below so that you can put your own comments in for the presentations you are about to observe.

❷ As you observe, think about the positive statements you could make using the examples.

❸ For each presentation, try to think of one way in which it might have been improved. Some examples are given for you.

Group A Focus: language choices

Positive	Point to improve
Used language really effectively to show the differences between the Lord and the child. The child's voice was noticeable because the group had used much simpler words.	The language of the Lord could have used even more complex sentences to show how educated he was.

Group B Focus: impact on audience

Positive	Point to improve
I thought the bit where both characters turned to each other and paused, as if they could see each other across all those miles, was really tense.	Perhaps if they had used more gesture and expression at times it could have improved the impact.

Group C Focus: different ways of addressing audience

Positive	Point to improve
The part where both voices were talking at the same time was really good because it was as if they weren't listening to each other and that's what happened in real life.	The child character didn't look at the audience but, maybe they were supposed to be shy. The adult character should have looked directly at us because she had power.

Group D Focus: characters, relationships and issues

Positive	Point to improve
The way it ended with the child silent and the adult still talking over them was great because it showed the complete power of adults over children. The children had no voice until now and they still can't really be heard.	I would like to see this on video because I think it would make a really powerful documentary.

Finding my voice

The characters you have created in this unit, the lost voices of the children and adults, have been created by you. But have you got your own voice? How confident is it? How can you develop your 'voice' so that you can speak out with confidence when you need to?

❶ After listening to your group's comments on your presentation and the others, work in pairs to help one another reflect critically on your work.

❷ Copy a blank version of the table below and think of three ways in which you could improve your writing (and speaking) of dramatic monologues in the future.

Self review of dramatic monologues		
Objective	**What I did well…**	**What I could do better…**
Making effective language choices	I used some really powerful and persuasive words for the adult	
Having impact on my audience		I think I would try to use more expression and eye contact in future
Experimenting with different ways of addressing my audience		Maybe I could talk more directly to them by using forms like, 'So you see, don't you?' as in rhetorical questions
Portraying characters, relationships and issues	I thought I really got across the pain my character was feeling by choosing emotional words like 'distraught'	

UNIT 5 The spelling troubleshooters

In this unit you will learn about the following key objectives:

Complex and unfamiliar words – ways of spelling complicated words which you have yet to master

Spelling strategies – which will extend and consolidate the range of spelling strategies that you already know

As Year 8 spellers you now have a wealth of experience behind you. Think of all those years learning to spell what once seemed difficult words but which you now find so simple. Spelling becomes easier because you learn strategies, ways to tackle difficult words, and you also become more familiar with how words should look.

The aim of this unit is to explore those strategies a little further. You can use the expertise you already have and develop it further. By the end of the unit, you really will be a fully-fledged spelling troubleshooter!

During the unit you will be designing and keeping your own spelling journal. In preparation for this, make a list of your 'top ten spelling strategies'. This will form the first page of your journal.

Dwight Douglas – teenage spelling champion!

Dwight Douglas is America's champion teen speller. He has just won the prestigious national spelling bee contest at the tender age of 12 by beating contestants many years his senior.

TASK

Read the article about Dwight Douglas and make a list of some effective spelling strategies.

The championships were held in Washington D.C. and were the culmination of a year's ferocious competition, with heats being held in most major towns and cities across the country. Dwight, a resident of Ohio, had to participate in 12 separate heats before eventually making it into the final as the youngest ever contender for the title.

Despite his hectic schedule Dwight found time to talk to this paper and enlighten us just how it was he could remain so cool and spell those words right every time.

Dwight felt that it was his grasp of spelling strategies that helped him secure the title: 'Ever since I began to learn to spell there are certain techniques I've relied upon, such as mnemonics and visualisation; they're my personal favourites'.

Asked to explain just exactly what he meant by this Dwight continued: 'Well, mnemonics are where you make

TASK

Working with a partner, predict the strategies that you think Dwight might have used to help him win the contest. Read on to see if you were right.

up a saying to help you remember a difficult spelling – you know, like necessary: you wear one collar and two sleeves – to remember one c and two s's. Visualising is where I can see the word in my head, the pattern it makes, or sometimes I see a picture, like with the word parallel – I imagine the two l's extended to help me remember they're there and it links with the meaning of the word having them opposite each other.'

TASK

Think of one other example of either mnemonics or visualisation.

Dwight also relies upon other strategies, such as looking for words within words: 'If I'm given a really long word to spell, that I've not heard before, I listen to see if it has any words I already know inside it. You know, a really simple example is 'believe' – it has the word 'lie' inside it.' Sometimes, when learning a word Dwight would say it aloud and over-emphasise the syllables or the sounds and that would help him:

'Take a word like separate. I'd say it in the wrong way – sep'ar'ate; it sounds silly, but it helps you remember'. But for every word, he relied upon: Look, Cover, Say, Write and Check – Dwight said it was ultimately the only way he could take in all of the words he had to learn.

Dwight is already preparing for next year's contest. Although now we all know his strategies he might find himself with more competition!

TASK

❶ Summarise, in a sentence, Dwight's winning technique and include each of his favourite strategies.

❷ You can see from the article about Dwight that there are numerous strategies to help you with your spelling. Some might already be familiar to you and others might seem unusual at first.

Review your own writing. This could be writing in English or any other subject. Find at least ten words which you commonly misspell. Then, use a copy of the table on the OHT to make an entry into your spelling journal. The left-hand side has points to consider about spelling. You can add others you may already know about or have researched in the empty spaces. On the right-hand side you can add words that you think you would use those strategies with, if you were trying to learn them. Make sure you have an example in each row.

Mastering mnemonics

The word 'mnemonic' is from the Greek word *mneme* meaning to remember. A mnemonic is any technique, such as a formula or a rhyme, that aids and jogs memory. Below are a few examples:

GEOGRAPHY: George eats old grey rats and paints houses yellow

ARITHMETIC: A rat in the house might eat the ice cream

CEMETERY: Remember it has three e's by imagining three headstones standing in a row

STATIONERY: remember 'e' for envelope, to remember this is how you spell the word when it is to do with paper

SEPARATE: Think of the 'r' in separate, as separating the two a's

BECAUSE: Babies eat carrots and Uncle Sam's eggs

NECESSARY: To remember that it is one 'c' and two 's', just say that it is necessary that you have one collar on your shirt but two sleeves. OR Not every cat eats sardines, shrimps and raspberry yoghurt

TASK

❶ Now create your own mnemonics for words that you find especially difficult. Remember that they are for your use so you can include references that are significant to you. Once completed this will be another page for your journal, providing you with your own mnemonic dictionary for all those hard-to-remember words.

❷ Choose three mnemonics from your list, learn the spellings and test yourself with your partner.

❸ Working in pairs, design a mnemonic for the word 'mnemonic' and use it as the title for your spelling journal page.

Spelling seminar

TASK

With all the expertise you have accumulated over the years and the resources you have gathered for your spelling journal, it is time for you to share some of that knowledge.

❶ Divide into groups of five. Each group will be experts on one of the strategies. In your groups, help each other to complete a copy of the 'Speech frame', so that each of you is an expert on that particular strategy.

❷ You are now going to disseminate that expertise to the rest of the group and teach others how to use your specialist strategy effectively.

Speech frame

1 Explain which spelling strategy you are going to talk about
- My specialist strategy will be 'words within words'
-

2 Give examples of the words it could be used with
- Sepa – rat – e
- Be – lie – ve
-

3 Say what you can find useful about the strategy
- I can remember simple words easily and this helps me to learn the bigger words
-

4 Explain when you think it might be useful
- I think it could be useful when I have to write quickly – like in an exam when I don't have my spelling journal with me
-

TASK

Make a note of three useful tips which came from the 'jigsaw' group. Use the 'Expert advice' page in your spelling journal.

Expert eye

Proofreading means checking written texts to ensure that they contain no mistakes; it simply means reading for errors. Your own work might be proofread by you or an independent reader such as a friend, parent or teacher. In fact, every piece of text you read in a printed form will be checked before you see it.

If you are going to ensure that your writing is of the highest quality, you need to become effective at proofreading.

TASK

Look at this example from a book trying to emulate the success of Harry Potter. It is riddled with mistakes. Proofread the passage and correct as many errors as you can in five minutes. Remember, proofreading is a skill which is often done under pressure of time. How quick and accurate can you be?

You might, for instance, proofread by using skimming skills. Sometimes a ruler or even the tips of your fingers can help to guide your eyes quickly along the lines. Decide what works best for you.

Henrietta Porter was hatted by the Durveys, the family that she had the misfortune to live with for the passed ten years, and there hatred might have destroyed her if it had not been for her atendance at Hogspots School.

Hogspots was the one saving grace of her existance with its collection of weird and wonderful teechers: ranging from wizards to goblins. The more time she spent their, the more proficient she became at concocting her own potions and casting her own spells. If only she could use them on the Durveys.

Often she would lie awake at knight, in her mind's eye she would be turning the pages in her spell book, imagining the consequences of each of the spells if they where to be enacted upon each of the dreadful Durveys. To turn them into toads or to visit upon them a plague of boils would just meen the wave of a wand and she would be free of them forever but unfortunatly Hogspots would not permit such exceses. If she were to act it would mean she would be expeled; condemned to life in the Muddle world and she could never had that!

TASK

❶ Compare your proofreading with a partner. Did you spot the same errors? Did you use the same skimming technique?

❷ Jot down your preferred technique on your 'Expert advice' page.

The Stone of Rosetta

The Stone of Rosetta is a compact basalt slab, found in July 1799 in the small Egyptian village called Rosette. It is now located in the British Museum in London.

The Stone contains three inscriptions of the same text: one in hieroglyphs; one in Demotic – everyday Egyptian script; one in Greek.

The other two languages on the Stone were known and this allowed the scholar Jean Francois Champollion to decipher the hieroglyphs. From this point the world had an understanding of Egyptian hieroglyphs never before available.

Clearly, Jean Francois was a highly intelligent man, but unfortunately when he came to write out the text in English he made a number of careless mistakes. He needs an expert to sort it out.

TASK

Imagine that you are scholars of the Egyptian world. You are about to publish the first translation of this ancient language to an eager body of scientists. Working in pairs, proofread the text below to ensure that it is perfect for publication. Remember it is an ancient and difficult language. Making sense of it will be a real challenge.

In the reign of the younge one who has suceded his father in the kingship, lord of diadems, most glorious, who has establisd Egipt and is pius towards the gods…

…he has directed that the gods shall continue to engoy the revenues of the temples and the yearly alowances given to them, both of corn and money, likewise allso the revenue asigned to the gods from the vine land and from gardens and the other propertys which beloged to the gods in his father's time… . He directed also, with regard to the preists, that they shuld pay no more…

The expert's journal

In this unit you have created at least two pages for your spelling journal; one on mnemonics and one on your list of top ten strategies. It is time for you to start compiling the remainder of the journal.

TASK

Each strategy needs its own page, just as you completed for the mnemonics. Write down the words for which you would use that strategy. This is something you can add to as you continue to develop your expertise.

Below is an example of how you might want to arrange your page.

- **Strategy:** visualisation

- **Strategy:** syllabification: re – mem – ber

- **Strategy:** calligram: a word picture Parallel..........(written with the two l's extended)

TASK

Look carefully at your spelling journal. Bearing in mind the number of strategies that Dwight managed to learn successfully, set yourself a challenge for the next three weeks. How many strategies and new words can you learn in that time?

Calligram: a word picture

UNIT 6 It's what's appropriate, innit!

KEY OBJECTIVES

In this unit you will learn about the following key objectives:

Informal to formal – the differences between informal and formal writing

Standard English and dialect – how the language of different regions is different to that used on the BBC news

Explain complex ideas – how to write explanations of difficult ideas or information

Evaluate own speaking – thinking about how you have developed as a speaker and how you could further improve

Listen for specific purpose – listening carefully and selecting relevant information for comment

Do you speak in the same way when you are with your friends as when you are with your teachers? With your parents as with your dentist? With a grandparent as with a baby brother or sister? The answer, unless you use language in a very peculiar way, is no.

People choose **formal** or **informal** language according to **context**. What is appropriate in one context may be inappropriate in another. Context means the situation or setting in which the language is being used. This unit explores the different ways people use spoken language, both formal and informal. It does not claim that there is a correct and incorrect way of speaking. Rather, it reflects on what is appropriate language in different contexts.

TASK

❶ Talk to a partner about what you have done today. You should talk as yourself. However, imagine your partner is first a friend, then a teacher, then a very small child.

❷ How did your speech vary each time your partner changed role? Why?

Formal and informal situations

There are accepted ways of behaving in every social situation we come across. In a formal situation the accepted way of behaving requires you to stay within quite narrowly defined boundaries. At other times the situations are informal and allow you more freedom with the ways you can behave.

Formality applies not just to language and behaviour but to the whole range of social activity: dressing, walking, eating, sitting.

TASK

❶ Working in pairs, place the situations illustrated below on a formality line. Highly informal scores 1; highly formal scores 10. Some of the situations will fall somewhere in between.

❷ Report back to the class on your findings.

A line of formality

⟵───────────────────────────────⟶

| I | 10 |
| Highly informal | Highly formal |

Each year at Christmas, the Queen delivers a speech for television and radio. She uses formal language and a formal tone of voice. People can vary the tone of their voice: for example, it is possible to sound sarcastic, angry or joyous.

TASK

Listen to a snippet of the Queen's speech and decide on an exact word or phrase to describe her tone of voice.

TASK

In the extract below, the 'Queen's speech' has somehow lost its appropriate formality. Each line has been written with a different audience in mind. Some of these audiences require a formal style, others an informal one. This could be to do with their age, their beliefs or their social background.

❶ In pairs, read the speech and identify the different audiences the lines have been written for. Pick out words and phrases that give you clues.

❷ Read the speech again, changing your tone of voice to suit each of the inappropriate audiences. How do you know which voice to use for which audience? What issues does this raise?

Biggin' it up to the UK Massive!

Ladies and Gentlemen

Are you sitting comfortably? Then I'll begin

Well I were just talking to me other half the other day and I says to him

Verily, this has been a mighty fine year

You listening at the back? I'm only going to say this once

The aforementioned UK has undertaken extensive improvements in public services

It is being really good that the schools is getting better exam results, innit?

MONSTER CASH INJECTION FOR HOSPITALS

And that was a stupendous piece of skill that put the Prime Minister clean through in her campaign to tidy up Britain's streets. Remarkable

A fine and successful year. It makes me proud to lead you all

Speaking patterns in the UK

So far you have looked at how the vocabulary, grammar and tone of both spoken and written language can vary according to context. People may also sound different when they speak, according to where they live or their social class. The term for the way someone pronounces words is **accent**.

TASK

It is often possible to tell where people come from in the UK by the accent with which they speak. Do you know the accents spoken in any of the places on the map below?

Glasgow
Belfast
Newcastle-upon-Tyne
Liverpool
Birmingham
Cardiff
London

Vocabulary

Accent: the features of pronunciation linked with a particular region or social class

Dialect: a distinctive variation of a language with its own vocabulary and grammatical constructions. It is often used in a particular region or by people of a similar social background

Standard English: the grammar and vocabulary of a dialect of English that has gained prestige and is now the most widely understood. It is used on the BBC news and taught in language schools around the world. Almost everything written in this book is written in Standard English

TASK

Listen to the recording of different speakers reading the same news item. The speakers come from the different cities shown on the map. Note your impressions of each accent on a copy of the table below.

Accent	Words that describe this accent
Newcastle (Geordie)	Lilting, melodic

All the speakers use exactly the same words. Only their accents vary. They all use the same formal dialect, known as Standard English.

TASK

❶ Look closely at the following sentences which all include non-standard dialect words or grammar:

> You're turning it far too slow.
> Give it me now, it ain't fair!
> Saturday afternoon, we was walking down the road very slow.
> But Miss, I got off of the bench when you said.
> You can't blame me, I never did nothing.
> Being on me tod had never gone through me head.
> That's what I does anyway, I just ignores her.
> Go to the park, is it?
> She be a right old barmpot.

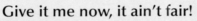

If you can think of further examples of non-standard dialect sentences, add them to a copy of the list.

❷ In pairs, rewrite each sentence in Standard English.

❸ Compare the non-standard dialect sentences with your Standard English versions. Which features of Standard English vary in a non-standard dialect?

❹ Report your findings to the rest of the class.

Speaking proper?

TASK

Listen again to the recording of the first person reading the news.
❶ Which part of the country do you think this person comes from?
❷ What do you think is the background of this person? Why?

 You might have guessed that the person is from the South of England. This is a possibility but not a certainty. This person has a **social** accent, not a **geographical** accent. In other words, their accent has more to do with their social background, especially their education, than where they live. This accent is associated with the South-East of England, but this does not mean it is a southern accent. Instead, it is an accent often used by people who have jobs linked to high levels of education, such as lawyers, doctors, bankers or teachers. Some people regard it as an accent that has particular prestige.

This type of accent is known as **Received Pronunciation** (RP). It is sometimes known by other names, such as Oxford English and BBC English. What do each of these names suggest?

TASK

Read the letter below, written to a newspaper.
❶ Summarise the letter's argument.
❷ Do you agree or disagree with the letter? Why?
❸ Do you think using RP is more formal or authoritative than speaking with a regional accent? Why?

Dear Sir/Madam,

I am writing in outrage at the use of a Yorkshire accent on the six o'clock national news. This is news for the whole country and, as such, should be read by a voice understood by all. I myself am no fan of Yorkshire folk and so find it off-putting to listen to such a voice when I am trying to hear important information about national and world affairs. End this nonsense immediately!

Colonel Ivor Grouch

A history of Standard English and Received Pronunciation

You should be starting to form opinions on the use of Standard English and Received Pronunciation. Read the history behind the two to see how they came into being.

Received Pronunciation (RP) and Standard English (SE) are often seen as the most correct forms of spoken and written language. This is not the case. No one form of language is more or less correct than any other. However, using them does suggest education can give people a certain status.

The roots of SE can be traced to 1476 when William Caxton introduced the printing press to Britain. At that time dialects of English were so varied that it was possible for two people from different areas to meet and not understand one another. Once text could be printed in large quantities, a standard language that all could understand started to evolve.

RP began to evolve a little later, about 400 years ago. The royal court in London was the place of most influence. Therefore, the accent used there was linked to power and status. People coming to London adopted the accent to appear powerful themselves.

Standard English developed most rapidly in the 18th century. Dr Johnson's dictionary was published in 1755 and in 1762 Robert Lowth completed A *Short Introduction to English Grammar*. Lowth invented rules that did not previously exist. It is because of him that 'different from' is deemed correct, while 'different to' and 'different than' are not!

RP spread further at the end of the 19th century when public schools such as Eton and Harrow became more popular. Pupils spoke RP to hide regional backgrounds and to show they were well educated. RP's influence grew stronger with the start of BBC radio broadcasts in the 1920s. RP speakers were used to avoid regional bias, but also because highly educated upper class or middle class people tended to get jobs at the BBC.

The RP spoken until the 1950s would sound 'posh' to a modern ear. As education became available to more people and popular culture, such as pop music, grew, so RP changed. Today RP still does not show where a speaker comes from, but it does not sound so 'posh'.

Standard English settled into something resembling its current form by the start of the 1800s. However, changes are always taking place. It is estimated that something like 15,000 new English words enter the language every year! All sorts of factors bring about these new words, such as immigration into Britain in the 1950s and 60s, the influence of the United States on popular culture and developments in computer technology.

❶ Using a copy of the extract above, highlight information about Standard English and dialect in one colour. Then use another colour to highlight everything to do with Received Pronunciation and accent.

❷ Using a timeline, plot information about dialect on one side, and accent on the other.

Attitudes to language use

It is time to decide exactly how you feel about the use of formal and informal language, the appropriateness of Standard English in different contexts and the use of different accents.

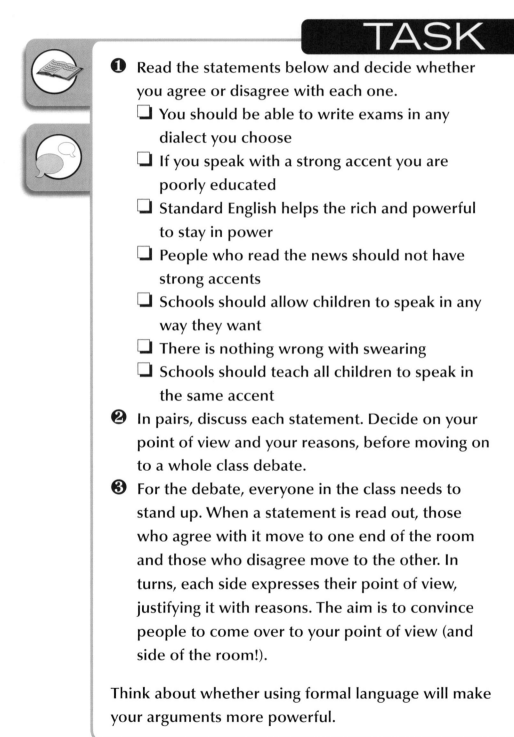

TASK

❶ Read the statements below and decide whether you agree or disagree with each one.
- ❏ You should be able to write exams in any dialect you choose
- ❏ If you speak with a strong accent you are poorly educated
- ❏ Standard English helps the rich and powerful to stay in power
- ❏ People who read the news should not have strong accents
- ❏ Schools should allow children to speak in any way they want
- ❏ There is nothing wrong with swearing
- ❏ Schools should teach all children to speak in the same accent

❷ In pairs, discuss each statement. Decide on your point of view and your reasons, before moving on to a whole class debate.

❸ For the debate, everyone in the class needs to stand up. When a statement is read out, those who agree with it move to one end of the room and those who disagree move to the other. In turns, each side expresses their point of view, justifying it with reasons. The aim is to convince people to come over to your point of view (and side of the room!).

Think about whether using formal language will make your arguments more powerful.

A personal language file

Did you know that you start to learn language before you are born? Babies in the womb can recognise the voice of their mother and those close to her. The learning process continues rapidly once you are born. Every aspect of your life has an impact on how you speak and view language use.

- Influence of friends
- TV and music
- Attitude to RP and other accents
- Attitude to dialects
- Attitude to SE
- Other influences

TASK

❶ Create a series of connecting boxes that make up your personal language file, like the ones below. Create and fill as many boxes as possible.

❷ Share all the different influences noted by members of your class. Make a wall display for your classroom.

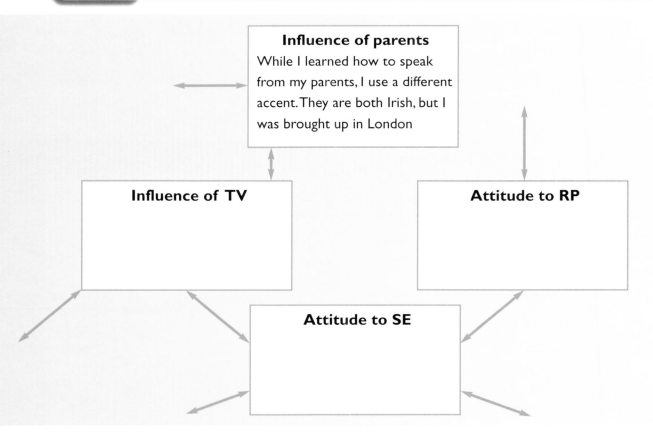

Influence of parents
While I learned how to speak from my parents, I use a different accent. They are both Irish, but I was brought up in London

Influence of TV

Attitude to RP

Attitude to SE

Respect to da informality!

Comedians have always played with language to create humour. Sacha Baron Cohen does just that with his comic creation, Ali G. The character of Ali is supposed to be a young British Asian male obsessed with Black gangster culture. He tries to speak, in his words, like a *gangsta-man*, but only ends up sounding stupid.

TASK

❶ Read out Ali's words below using an RP accent. Why does this sound wrong?

❷ How many examples of non-standard grammar can you find in this short passage? What effect does this produce?

▌▌ Wicked! I is here with none other than Tony Benn. He been in the political game f[or] many, many years. So nobody know it as he does, and he is going to explain wh[at] the socialism is and what all the left stuff is going on. What is socialism, Tony? ▌▌

This passage starts a longer interview with Tony Benn. Tony Benn is a well-known Labour politician with strongly held views about socialism. Ali G regularly interviews older people on television who do not know who he is. While he uses language in a comical way, it is often the guests who end up looking foolish because they are unsure how to react to a young person using, what is for them, very unfamiliar language.

TASK

❶ Listen to the recording of Ali G interviewing Tony Benn.

❷ Why exactly is this interview funny?

❸ How well do you think Tony Benn copes with Ali G's questions?

But why is it funny?

Analysing comedy does not necessarily make it any funnier. However, it is an excellent way to see exactly how language works.

TASK

Listen to the Ali G recording again, this time taking notes on a copy of the table below:

Type of informality	Examples
Using a word only featured in young people's dialect	wicked
Using a slang word or phrase	jiggy
Using an offensive word	
Non-standard subject-verb link (e.g. saying 'she gone' instead of 'she went')	
Non-standard use of pronoun (e.g. using 'him' instead of 'he')	
Non-standard word order in a sentence	

TASK

❶ In pairs, decide on a way of speaking that has comic potential – either because it is too formal or informal for its context.

❷ Role play conversations between any of the following: a taxi driver, a judge, a check-out operator, a police officer, a teacher, a pupil, a doctor, a builder, a politician.

❸ Write a short dialogue of about 200 words taking place between two of your choices.

As formal as it gets

There are some occasions when nothing but the most formal language will do, for example when making a speech at a formal meeting or preparing a talk for a radio station in order to put forward a particular point of view.

TASK

Below is a script for one part of a radio programme in which guest speakers present their views on topical issues in a formal way.

❶ Analyse the features of the script. What makes it both formal and powerfully worded?

❷ Using a copy of the script, highlight interesting words and phrases, and annotate with comments about the effect produced.

It is my contention that school holidays must be extended from six to ten weeks.

Children today have less and less time for fun, less and less time for play, less and less time to explore the world away from the influence of adults.

Exhausted children sit slumped at the back of classrooms around the country as the final term of the school year drags to a close. Their brains can take being force-fed no more.

Furthermore, it is not only the children who are suffering, but their teachers too.

How many tempers snap in those final few weeks of term? How many mild-mannered misters and misses explode because they have had too much?

There are those who believe that the holidays should be shorter, not longer. Sadistic headteachers yearn to keep pupils within their grasp for as long as possible, cramming them ever more full with exam-driven facts. Under no circumstances must this happen. Exams will never be passed if there is insufficient time for relaxation and pleasure.

Longer, not shorter. That is my message.

Let us join together in setting children free and releasing them from those who would suck all the fun from young lives.

In an orderly and formal fashion

It is not just word choice and word order that makes a spoken text formal. The order in which it is written also plays a part. The script you have just considered has deliberately been organised as a series of sections or **chunks**. This has made the point of view clearer and more powerful.

TASK

❶ Look at the chunks below. Notice how they match the sections of the script about school holidays.

```
┌─────────────────────────────────────────┐      ┌──────────────────────┐
│ Assertion (establishing point of view)   │─────▶│ Main argument for    │──┐
└─────────────────────────────────────────┘      └──────────────────────┘  │
                                                                            │
┌──────────┐      ┌──────────────────────────┐      ┌──────────┐           │
│ Evidence │◀─────│ Another important argument │◀────│ Evidence │◀──────────┘
└──────────┘      └──────────────────────────┘      └──────────┘
     │
     │  ┌────────────────────┐      ┌──────────┐      ┌─────────────────────┐
     └─▶│ Refuting objections │─────▶│ Summary │─────▶│ Appeal to the listener │
        └────────────────────┘      └──────────┘      └─────────────────────┘
```

❷ Use the same chunks to plan your own short, formal script for a school or local radio station, expressing a point of view. You could write about one of the following topics or choose your own:
- ❏ English lessons should be taught to single sex groups
- ❏ Chewing gum should be banned in all public places
- ❏ Cars should be banned from all town centres
- ❏ All teachers and pupils should call each other by their Christian names

❸ Once you are happy with your plan, write your script and record it for the radio station.

❹ As you listen to each recording, note comments or questions about the speaker's point of view. Make these points to the speaker after each recording.

❺ Write an evaluation of your radio performance, bringing out what you did well and what you could have done better. At the same time, think more widely about your ability as a speaker. What are your strengths as a speaker? What could you improve?

Designing a leaflet

You are going to design a leaflet aimed at young people of your own age. Its purpose is to provide information about language and explain clearly how it varies in different contexts. The leaflet should be written in a formal style but be lively enough to appeal to your age group.

TASK

Look back through this unit and the work you have done. Produce a diagram like the one below, noting all the key ideas and issues about language that you have come across. Each of these will become a paragraph or section in your leaflet.

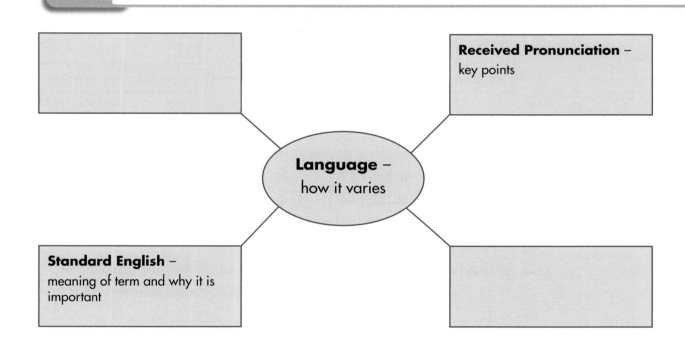

Received Pronunciation – key points

Language – how it varies

Standard English – meaning of term and why it is important

TASK

❶ Once you have gathered ideas, share your diagram with a partner. Add or delete ideas as required.

❷ Your leaflet should be A4 in size and folded into three sections. This means you will have six panels to complete. Use a planning sheet to map out what will go where in your leaflet. Do not start the actual writing yet.

Becoming a style guru

There are plenty of imaginative tricks of the writing style trade that you should consider using in your leaflet. What would you add to the following tips?

Sensible sequence

Make sure your leaflet is well organised so that your reader does not get confused. For example, have sections on formal and informal language together, likewise Standard English and dialect.

Tempting titles

Use catchy titles and sub-titles to clearly inform the reader what comes next and keep his or her interest.

Explain yourself

The ideas you are writing about are quite complex so it is vital that you are crystal clear. Use some of the following techniques in each section:

- Signpost what the section is about, e.g. Next…, Also important is…, Another key area…
- Use short, sharp sentences for key points
- Use connectives such as 'because' to explain ideas, e.g. Formal language is important because…
- Provide definitions of key words
- Include examples to illuminate points
- Include comparisons, e.g. Unlike…, In contrast…, In the same way…
- Use rhetorical questions followed by answers, e.g. So what exactly is dialect? Dialect can be defined as…

Beautiful bullets

Consider summing up key points in bullet points

Be fussy about formal

● Avoid first person statements such as 'I don't like accents that are from the South of England.' This is not about what you do and don't like! To be more formal, use the third person, e.g. 'Some people have prejudices against certain accents'.

● You can also use passive constructions to avoid the first person, e.g, 'Standard English can be defined as…' NOT 'I would define Standard English as…'

● Use the correct terminology, e.g. accent, dialect

● Use formal vocabulary, e.g. 'It is in your own interests to think carefully about…' NOT 'You'd be seen as thick if you…'

● Use nominalisation. In other words, try turning verbs into nouns, e.g. Instead of writing 'Exam results <u>were rising</u> rapidly, which pleased teachers', write 'The <u>rapid rise</u> in exam results pleased teachers'.

Fabulous fonts

If you are using a computer, select a font that is appropriate for your audience and purpose.

Times New Roman probably makes you a traditionalist.

Comic Sans shows a sense of humour.

Dorchester Script would be inappropriate.

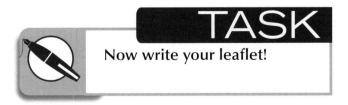

TASK

Now write your leaflet!

The Language Variations

Lauren Thorpe 8C

In this unit you will learn about the following key objectives:

Prepositions and connectives – learning how to extend the range of prepositions and connectives you use to link ideas in your writing

Grouping sentences – exploring and comparing different ways of grouping sentences in your paragraphs so that your ideas are clear and well developed

Development of key ideas – analysing the structure of a whole text in order to identify how the writer develops key ideas

Develop an argument – learning how to write a formal argument in a way which makes it easy for the reader to follow your ideas

In this unit you will study the techniques that have been used by successful speakers to present their views persuasively to an audience. By studying selected speeches you will learn how to select, organise and express your ideas, feelings and attitudes in ways that will influence your listeners. At the end of the unit you will write your own persuasive speech on a chosen topic.

Features of persuasive speeches

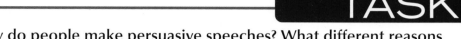

❶ Why do people make persuasive speeches? What different reasons do they have for making them? With a partner, think of five different sorts of people who make persuasive speeches. Think of their reasons for doing so. Compile a class list.

❷ Before you begin to read some persuasive speeches, discuss what you already know about the features of persuasive argument.

❸ Draw up a list of features with a partner before you share ideas with your class. You should think about:
   ❏ How the ideas are organised and sequenced
   ❏ What sort of sentences are used and how they are connected
   ❏ What sort of vocabulary is used

Important features of persuasive argument and speeches

● The text begins by introducing the topic for argument and ends by concluding that argument
● The ideas are organised in a logical sequence of paragraphs
● Each paragraph is built around a point and an elaboration of that point
● The writer/speaker addresses his/her listeners
● Facts may be used to support arguments, but opinions can also be used
● Connectives are used to suggest logical links
● The present tense is generally used
● Short, simple sentences are used for emphasis
● Longer, complex sentences are used to convey strong feelings or build crucial arguments
● Adjectives and adverbs are used for impact
● Exaggerated statements, rhetorical questions and exclamations are used for emotive and rhetorical effect
● Words or groups of words are repeated, often in noticeable patterns

---

Though many good persuasive speeches share some of these key features, all great speeches will have their own special qualities, as you will discover.

TASK

The following speakers clearly feel passionately about the subjects on which they speak. With a partner, discuss which issues might prompt you to make a persuasive speech.

The first two speeches that you will study were both delivered by American women in the nineteenth century and illustrate how women at this time battled to convince others that women were equal to men. The first speaker, Sojourner Truth, was a black American slave. Her speech, delivered at the Women's Convention in Akron, Ohio in 1851, argues her case for equal rights with men. She would originally have been speaking in an American dialect.

TASK

As you read the text below for the first time, consider whether you would have been convinced by Sojourner Truth's argument and why.

Ain't I a woman?

Well, children, where there is so much racket there must be something out of kilter. I think that twixt the Negroes of the South and the women at the North, all talking about rights, the white men will be in a fix pretty soon. But what's all this here talking about?

That man over there says that women need to be helped into carriages, and lifted over ditches, and to have the best place everywhere. Nobody ever helps me into carriages, or over mud-puddles, or gives me any best place! And ain't I a woman? Look at me! Look at my arm! I have ploughed and planted, and gathered into barns, and no man could head me! And ain't I a woman? I could work as much and eat as much as a man – when I could get it – and bear the lash as well! And ain't I a woman? I have borne thirteen children, and seen most all sold off to slavery, and when I cried out with my mother's grief, none but Jesus heard me! And ain't I a woman?...

Then that little man in black there, he says women can't have as much rights as men, 'cause Christ wasn't a woman? Where did your Christ come from? Where did your Christ come from? From God and a woman! Man had nothing to do with Him.

If the first woman God ever made was strong enough to turn the world upside down all alone, these women together ought to be able to turn it back, and get it right side up again! And now they is asking to do it, the men better let them.

❶ Briefly discuss your first responses to Sojourner Truth's speech with a partner, before sharing ideas with the class. You should consider:
- ☐ The ideas that she is expressing
- ☐ The way she argues her viewpoint
- ☐ The language used by Sojourner Truth and its effectiveness – check the list on page 130

❷ Working in small groups, use the handout to record the features of this speech. Remember to select some words and phrases from the speech that illustrate the language features on page 130 and think about why they are effective. The first paragraph has been done for you.

Paragraph	A good title for this paragraph would be?	Language features	Words or phrases to illustrate	Reasons for effectiveness
Paragraph 1	What is everyone talking about?	Colloquial language	'Well, children, where there is so much racket…'	Speaks directly to ordinary people in her own language
		A question	'But what's all this here talking about?'	Makes audience want to hear the answer

The right to vote

The second speaker is Susan B. Anthony. She was arrested for voting illegally in the American presidential election of 1872. At that time no woman had the right to vote. In this speech, she argues forcefully that she has as much right to vote as any man.

TASK

As you read the text, trace the argument, as you did with the previous text. You should be able to identify the topic sentences for each paragraph of this speech. You will notice that, unlike Sojourner Truth, Susan B. Anthony speaks in a legal register. On first reading you may find some of her vocabulary unfamiliar. You will be asked to consider the meaning of the underlined words in their context, before checking them in a dictionary.

Friends and fellow citizens: I stand before you tonight under <u>indictment</u> for the <u>alleged crime</u> of having voted at the last presidential election, without having a lawful right to vote. It shall be my work this evening to prove to you that in thus voting, I not only committed no crime, but, instead, simply exercised my citizen's rights, guaranteed to me and all United States citizens by the National Constitution, beyond the power of any state to deny.

The <u>preamble</u> of the Federal Constitution says: 'We, the people of the United States, in order to form a more perfect union, establish justice, insure domestic <u>tranquillity</u>, provide for the common defence, promote the general welfare, and secure the blessings of liberty to ourselves and our <u>posterity</u>, do ordain and establish this Constitution for the United States of America.'

It was we, the people, not we, the white male citizens; nor yet we, the male citizens; but we, the whole people, who formed the Union. And we formed it, not to give the blessings of liberty, but to secure them; not to the half of ourselves and the half of our posterity, but to the whole people – women as well as men. And it is a downright <u>mockery</u> to talk to women of their enjoyment of the blessings of liberty while they are denied the use of the only means of securing them provided by this <u>democratic-republican</u> government – the ballot.

For any state to make sex a qualification that must ever result in the <u>disenfranchisement</u> of one entire half of the people, is to pass a bill of attainder, or, an <u>ex post facto law</u>, and is therefore a violation of the supreme law of the land. By it the blessings of liberty are forever withheld from women and their female posterity.

The only question left to be settled now is: Are women persons? And I hardly believe any of our opponents will have the hardihood to say they are not. Being persons, then, women are citizens; and no state has a right to make any law, or to enforce any old law, that shall abridge their privileges or immunities. Hence, every <u>discrimination</u> against women in the constitution and laws of the several states is today null and void, precisely as is every one against Negroes.

❶ Working with a partner, remind each other of ways to work out the meaning of unknown words. Copy the chart below and record what you think is the meaning of each of the underlined words in the Susan B. Anthony speech. Use a dictionary to check.

Word	We think it means	We worked it out by	Dictionary definition
Indictment			
Preamble			

❷ Discuss your response to the text with your class. You should consider:
   ❏ The effectiveness of the opening paragraph
   ❏ The way Susan B. Anthony uses legal language
   ❏ The features of her speech which might convince her audience that she had not broken the law

❸ In groups, use your handout to record the features of the speech.

❶ In your groups, discuss the similarities and differences between the speeches of Sojourner Truth and Susan B. Anthony. You should consider:
   ❏ The ideas in the speeches
   ❏ The ways the speakers use language to persuade
   ❏ The effectiveness of the speeches

❷ Now compose one sentence based on your discussion. You will be able to express your ideas more clearly if you use comparative and causal connectives, for example:

   Whilst Sojourner Truth uses colloquial expression **in order** to engage her audience, Susan B. Anthony speaks formally in legal language **so that** she is able to communicate her intelligence and knowledge.

❸ Share your sentence with the rest of the class.

Planning your own speech

❶ You are now going to plan a speech of your own. Choose one of the following topics:

❑ Your sports team at school is entering an important and challenging competition. Write a speech to persuade them that they can win.

❑ Year 8 pupils are to lose their valued common room. Write a speech to persuade your year head that this is the wrong decision.

❑ Your class wants to go on an outward bound course as part of your school's activities week. Your form tutor is not convinced. Write a speech arguing your case.

❷ In planning your ideas, you should think about:

❑ Your audience

❑ Your main argument

❑ The points in your argument

❑ Your elaboration of those points

❑ The type and patterns of language that will be most persuasive

❸ Use a copy of the planning grid below to organise your ideas.

Topic	Outward bound course
Main argument – **state in introduction**	Will be good for team building and increase independence amongst pupils
Audience and purpose **Suitable register, tone and pronouns**	Some of 8D. Form tutor. Not too casual, but use some conversational expressions
Points	
1	
2	
3	
Language features to be used	Patterns of three – to build emotion Rhetorical questions – to increase guilt

The use of metaphor in speeches

What do you know about metaphors and their use? A metaphor describes one thing as another. The effect of a metaphor is to make ideas more vivid. You will probably be more familiar with metaphors used in poems and narratives, but metaphor is also a powerful tool for the persuasive speaker. For example, when Sojourner Truth said women could 'turn the world upside down' she did not mean women could literally tip the planet over. She was using a metaphor to emphasise her feelings. Her metaphor was in tune with the rest of her speech – to emphasise the power of women to accomplish tremendous deeds.

TASK

❶ Identify the metaphors in these extracts, taken from famous speeches:
  ❑ South Africa… a rainbow nation at peace with itself
  ❑ The moment to bridge the chasms that divide us has come
  ❑ Never again… shall this beautiful land… suffer the indignity of being the skunk of the world
  ❑ We shall prove ourselves able… to ride out the storm of war
  ❑ Let Hitler bear his responsibilities to the full, and let the peoples of Europe who groan beneath his yoke aid in every way the coming of the day when that yoke will be broken
❷ Why have these speakers chosen these metaphors?
❸ How have the metaphors made the ideas more powerful?
❹ Choose one metaphor and present it visually for class display

The case for the space race

The next text to consider is part of a speech made in 1962 by President John F. Kennedy, the American President at that time. He delivered the speech to the university governors, scientists and teachers, politicians, and other distinguished guests at Rice University, Houston, Texas. In the first part of his speech President Kennedy outlines the swift progress of people in the previous half century. In the extracts you will read, he argues the case for America to explore space.

TASK

As you read this first extract, make a note of the words and phrases that impress you and persuade you of the value of space exploration. And notice those metaphors!

Man, in his quest for knowledge and progress, is determined and cannot be deterred. The exploration of space will go ahead, whether we join in or not, and it is one of the greatest adventures of all time, and no nation which expects to be the leader of other nations can expect to stay behind in this race for space.

Those who came before us made certain that this country rode the first waves of the industrial revolution, the first waves of modern invention, and the first wave of nuclear power, and this generation does not intend to founder in the backwash of the coming age of space. We mean to be part of it – we mean to lead it. For the eyes of the world now look into space, to the moon and to the planets beyond, and we have vowed that we shall not see it governed by a hostile flag of conquest, but by the banner of freedom and peace. We have vowed that we shall not see space filled with weapons of mass destruction, but with instruments of knowledge and understanding.

Yet the vows of this Nation can only be fulfiled if we in this Nation are first, and, therefore, we intend to be first. In short, our leadership in science and industry, our hopes or peace and security, our obligations to ourselves as well as others, all require us to make this effort, to solve these mysteries, to solve them for the good of all men and become the world's leading space-faring nation.

TASK

❶ Share first responses to this text with your class, before studying it in detail. How has Kennedy persuaded us that space exploration is important?

❷ Read and study this text again in close detail, looking at Kennedy's use of language – notice particularly how he employs metaphor.

Fly to the moon

TASK

Working in small groups, study the next extract from the same speech. How does Kennedy extend his central metaphor?

We set sail on this new sea because there is new knowledge to be gained, and new right to be won, and they must be won and used for the progress of all people. For space science, like nuclear science and all technology, has no conscience of its own. Whether it will become a force for good or ill depends on man, and only if the United States occupies a position of pre-eminence can we help decide whether this new ocean will be a sea of peace or a terrifying theatre of war. I do not say that we should or will go unprotected against the hostile misuse of space any more than we go unprotected against the hostile use of land or sea, but I do say that space can be explored and mastered without feeding the fires of war, without repeating the mistakes that man has made in extending his writ around this globe of ours.

There is no strife, no prejudice, no national conflict in outer space as yet. Its hazards are hostile to us all. Its conquest deserves the best of all mankind, and its opportunity for peaceful cooperation may never come again. But why, some say, the moon? Why choose this as our goal? And they may well ask why climb the highest mountain? Why 35 years ago, fly the Atlantic?…

It is for these reasons that I regard the decision last year to shift our efforts in space from low to high gear as among the most important decisions that will be made during my incumbency in the office of the Presidency…

We choose to go to the moon. We choose to go to the moon in this decade and do other things, not because they are easy, but because they are hard, because that goal will serve to organise and measure the best of our energies and skills, because that challenge is one that we are willing to accept, one we are unwilling to postpone, and one which we intend to win, and the others, too.

After you have read Kennedy's speech on page 138, answer the following questions:

❶ How does Kennedy use connectives and sentence grouping in his speech?

❷ What effect do you think this might have on an audience?

❸ Study the final two paragraphs of Kennedy's speech printed below. Do you think they give his speech a satisfying and effective conclusion? Give reasons for your decision.

Many years ago the great British explorer George Mallory, who was to die on Mount Everest, was asked why he wanted to climb it. He said, 'Because it is there.'

Well, space is there, and we're going to climb it, and the moon and the planets are there, and new hopes for knowledge and peace are there. And, therefore, as we sail we ask God's blessing on the most hazardous and dangerous and greatest adventure on which man has ever embarked.

TASK

Using the topic you chose to plan your own speech, discuss with a partner some of the words and phrases you could use for a dramatic and effective conclusion using the following language features:

● A metaphor
● Emotive words and phrases
● Carefully grouped and patterned sentences
● Logical connectives to add force to your argument

TASK

You will now work in groups to explore extracts from three famous speeches delivered by:

● Chief Seattle
● Tony Blair
● Winston Churchill

For each speech, you should consider:

● Its purpose
● The context in which it was delivered
● Its audience
● The way it is organised
● Its language features at word and sentence level
● Its effectiveness

We will fight them on the beaches

In May 1940, the British army fighting against the Germans in France during the Second World War, were driven back to Dunkirk. A mass evacuation from Dunkirk, made possible by heroic national effort, enabled over 338,000 Allied troops to reach England safely. The British celebrated the success of the evacuation. In June 1940, Winston Churchill, the British Prime Minister, delivered this speech to The House of Commons:

Turning once again to the question of invasion, there has, I will observe, never been a period in all those long centuries of which we boast when an absolute guarantee against invasion, still less against serious raids, could have been given to our people. In the days of Napoleon the same wind which might have carried his transports across the Channel might have driven away a blockading fleet. There is always the chance, and it is that chance which has excited and befouled the imaginations of many continental tyrants.

* * *

I have, myself, full confidence, that if all do their duty, if nothing is neglected, and if the best arrangements are made, as they are being made, we shall prove ourselves once again able to defend our Island home, to ride out the storm of war, and to outlive the menace of tyranny, if necessary for years, if necessary alone.

* * *

We shall not flag nor fail. We shall go on to the end. We shall fight in France, we shall fight on the seas and oceans; we shall fight with growing confidence and growing strength in the air; we shall defend our Island, whatever the cost may be; we shall fight on the beaches, we shall fight on the landing grounds, we shall fight in the fields and in the streets, we shall fight in the hills. We shall never surrender, and even if, which I do not for a moment believe, this Island or a large part of it were subjugated and starving, then our Empire beyond the seas, armed and guarded by the British Fleet, would carry on the struggle, until, in God's time, the New World, with all its power and might, steps forth to the liberation and rescue of the old.

How can we sell our land?

In 1854, the American President offered $150,000 to the native American tribes in North West America for 2 million acres of land, promising them a reservation in return. The following speech is a translation of the reply to that offer by Chief Seattle, chief of the Suquamish tribe.

The President in Washington sends word that he wishes to buy our land. But how can you buy or sell the sky, the land? The idea is strange to us. If we do not own the presence of the air and the sparkle of the water, how can you buy them?

Every part of this earth is sacred to my people. Every shining pine needle. Every sandy shore. Every mist in the dark woods. Every meadow. Every humming insect. All are holy in the memory and experience of my people. We know the sap that courses through the trees as we know the blood that courses through our veins.

* * *

The shining water that moves in the streams and rivers is not just water but the blood of our ancestors. If we sell you our land you must remember that it is sacred. Each ghostly reflection in the clear water of the lakes tells of events and memories in the life of my people. The water's murmur is the voice of my father's father.

* * *

So if we sell you our land, you must keep it apart and sacred as a place where man can go to taste the wind that is sweetened by the meadow flowers. Will you teach your children what we have taught our children, that the earth is our mother? What befalls the earth befalls all the sons of the earth. This we know. The earth does not belong to man, man belongs to the earth.

Britain can be better

Shortly before the 1997 General Election, the following speech was delivered by Tony Blair as a party political broadcast.

Look the Tories didn't get everything wrong in the eighties, let's just be honest about that, admit it. But Britain can be better, we can make this country better than it is.

* * *

Ask yourself this question: if these Tories get back in for another five years, will we even have a National Health Service in the way that we've known it, and grown up with it? Now we've got to rebuild the National Health Service, and as a start we will spend a hundred million pounds by cutting that bureaucracy, and putting it into cutting waiting lists.

Why should people in this country have to put up with these levels of crime? The fear, the abuse, the hassle, elderly people often afraid to go out of their own homes, sometimes afraid to be in their own home. The Labour party will take on this issue in every single aspect of it. Tough on crime, tough on the causes of crime.

* * *

Education is the future for this country. If we don't give our kids the right education they don't succeed, Britain doesn't succeed. That's why I've said, for a Labour government, its top three priorities: education, education, education. And again we can make a start, for example by reducing class sizes for all five, six and seven year olds in our primary schools to thirty or under. That we will do in the five years of a Labour government.

Britain can be better. We can make this country better than it is, and I am not going to promise anything that I can't deliver, but I do tell you that today's Labour party, transformed as it is with the strength of leadership and the strength of unity behind it, can make this country better.

❶ Choose one of the three speeches and practise reading a short section of it aloud.

❷ Present your feedback on one speech to the rest of the class.

❸ What three things have you learnt from this work that will influence you in writing your own speech to argue a case?

Delivering a speech

The following list provides some suggestions for a speaker who is preparing to deliver a speech. Can you add any more suggestions to the list?

- Stand straight and keep still while you speak
- Look at your audience, not at your notes
- Use some simple, appropriate hand gestures
- Pause between important ideas
- Vary your tone of voice and your pace as you speak
- Increase the volume of your voice at key moments
- Dwell on the key emotive words and phrases
- Allow your facial expression to convey emotion
- Pause at the end to let your message sink in

TASK

You are now going to write your own persuasive speech. Review all you have learnt about persuasive speeches before you begin. You should already have:

- Planned your speech
- Thought about a conclusion

Now you will need to:

- Research ideas for your speech
- Re-draft your speech as you develop ideas
- Think carefully about your audience and the purpose of your speech

Your speech will be assessed on its success in using the features of persuasive argument that you have studied.

TASK

❶ Make a note of the three most important things that you have learnt about speech-making in this unit.

❷ Which of the speeches that you have studied impressed you most? Why?

❸ How might the work you have done in this unit assist you in your other curriculum subjects?

Your work will be assessed in a number of ways throughout Key Stage 3. For example:

- Your teacher might talk to you about your work and suggest ways in which you might improve it

- You might be asked to work with a partner to make constructive comments about each other's drafted work

- You might be asked as a class to comment on a group presentation given by members of your class

- You might be set a test which will be marked by your teacher

- You might be asked to record some of your recent spelling errors and then think of strategies to learn those words which you find difficult

- Your teacher might write a comment at the end of a piece of work that you have done

It is very important, however, that you are fully involved in your own learning. You need to think about your strengths as a reader, writer and speaker and listener. You also need to think about areas which you need to improve. You need to be involved in the process of setting targets which will help you and your teacher to enable you to make progress in certain areas. This unit focuses on this process.

Making progress as a reader

A reading autobiography

Under 5 yrs   I had a plastic book which made lots of different noises. I remember having picture books which Dad read to me

5 yrs   I don't remember actually learning to read. We followed a reading scheme at school – I remember different coloured books

6 yrs   Reading lots at home. Always read in bed before I went to sleep. Still got my collection of *Stormy Night* books

7 yrs   Starting reading comics – Mum bought me the *Beano* every week. Not reading so many books now

8 yrs   Went to see film of *Stuart Little*. Read the book straight after. Loved it

9 yrs   Discovered Jacqueline Wilson – read all her books and began sharing and swapping books with friends. Joined a book club at school

10 yrs   Enjoyed the *Horrible History* series. Realised that I quite enjoyed non-fiction. Got a computer with my brother and started to surf the internet

11 yrs   Read *Stop the Train* in English. Tried *The Kite Rider* by the same author but found it quite difficult

12 yrs   Reading *Holes* in class. I enjoy working in small groups reading and talking about books. Just started *I am the Cheese*

In order to set yourself targets to improve your reading, you might like to think about your development as a reader over time.

Ask yourself the following questions:

- Where have I come from as a reader?

- Where am I now as a reader?

- Where do I want to be as a reader and how can I get there?

TASK

Draw a timeline like the one on page 147 which charts your own reading autobiography.

This timeline reader has had some very positive reading experiences. However, the pupils below are struggling with their reading.

TASK

Work with a partner as agony aunts. What advice would you give the following readers?

I really enjoyed the *Point Horror* books but I've read them all and don't know what else to read. I don't really enjoy anything else…
(Mark)

I don't see the point in reading when I can just watch TV instead…
(Roy)

I'm a really slow reader. By the time I get to the end of a book I've forgotten how it started…
(Carol)

I used to enjoy reading when I was younger but all the books I'm given now are boring…
(Kalia)

Books are expensive and I never know where to look in the library…
(Ali)

Making progress as a writer

Joanna produced the piece of writing below in response to the following task:

We all have a responsibility to take care of our environment. Write an article for your school magazine which aims to persuade your readers that this statement is true.

[sic.] We all need to take responsability for looking after our enviourment. Because if we dont our ancestors will suffer with pollution and global warming.

Our planet will flood from global warming if we dont react now.

Animals and birds could choke or get tangled up in our litter so always use a bin!

Imagine you were a seagull and you flew down to the beach to eat a bit of bread and when you flew off you realised you couldn't because you had fishing line rapped round your legs. How would you fell?

You can help by recycling your rubbish because rubbish just gets buried which contaminates the land and gets into our water system which makes us ill.

If you recycle you will stop them from buriying it and it can be used again.

Don't buy products tested on animals as it is wrong.

If you drop or see a pice of litter pick it up and put it in a dustbin so it dosn't harm animals.

If you need to go to your local shop walk or ride a bike. Don't use a car when you don't have to.

Simple things like picking up litter, recycling and walk instead of driving can help save our precious enviourment!

Read Joanna's work carefully,
making a note of:
- Three things she does well
- Two things she needs to improve

What has Joanna done well?

- Her writing has a clear introduction and conclusion

- She has plenty of interesting ideas

- She appeals directly to the reader and uses a rhetorical question

- She uses quite a good range of vocabulary

What could she do to improve her writing?

- She could develop her paragraphs

- She could check her spelling – the word 'environment' was printed in the question

- She could revise the rule for using apostrophes to join words

- She could vary the way she starts her sentences

TASK

Rewrite Joanna's work for her. Try especially to:
- Develop the ideas in each paragraph so that each one has a topic sentence which is developed throughout the rest of the paragraph. Make sure that all the ideas are organised logically too.
- Vary the way you begin your sentences, for example, you might begin a sentence with a subordinate clause, an adverb or a prepositional phrase.

Making progress as a speaker and listener

What sort of skills do you need to be successful in:

● Speaking?

● Listening?

TASK

❶ Use the following table to gather your ideas. It has been started for you.

Speaking	Listening
● Be aware of your listeners or audience	● Listen carefully to what other people say and build on their ideas
●	●
●	●
●	●

❷ At a recent parents' evening, your teacher makes the observations shown on page 152 about pupils in your class. For each pupil note down:
  ❏ Two or three strengths as a speaker and listener
  ❏ Two targets which will help him or her to be a better speaker and listener

Shamil is very quiet in class. She has plenty of good ideas but does not always feel confident enough to share them in class. She works better in small groups where she collaborates effectively and is able to draw others into the discussion.

Paul has been an active member of the debating club and he is very confident. He always has a contribution to make in class. Sometimes he answers questions without thinking through his ideas however and he doesn't always seem very interested in what others say.

Kyle is a very thoughtful speaker and he listens with sensitivity to others. He recently gave a very powerful speech to the class on animal cruelty. However, he tends to speak in a very chatty and informal way, even when the situation calls for something far more formal.

SMART targets

Specific

A vague target such as 'I want to be a better speaker and listener' will not help you. Make your targets specific, for example, 'I will listen more carefully to others in the group and respond to their ideas thoughtfully.'

Measurable

How will you know whether you have achieved your target? A specific target such as 'I will try to make a spoken contribution to every English lesson' will be easy to measure. Your teacher will also be able to help you.

Achievable

Make sure that you do not set yourself targets that are beyond your reach at the moment. Take things a step at a time. If you are a Level 4 speaker and listener and you want to be Level 6 next month, that is probably a little unrealistic; you will end up feeling demotivated. Set your sights just a little higher than where you are at the moment.

Relevant

Make sure that the target you set yourself is appropriate for you. Do not aim to improve your group contributions if it is really individual presentations that you are struggling with.

Time-bonded

We are all very good at putting things off and there are some jobs that just never seem to get done! Make sure that you set yourself a reasonable time limit, for example, 'By Easter I will have made regular spoken contributions in English at least once a week.'

Remember – be SMART!